ADVANCE PRAISE

"This book should be the cornerstone of every organization's growth strategy. At a time of unprecedented expectations, leaders need Batlaw's & Charan's unparalleled expertise and firsthand knowledge of how to place talented leaders for the best results. Outstanding!"

—BOB SWAN, former CEO, Intel Corporation

"Valuing talent has always been central to General Atlantic's investment process and success. Anish and Ram have taken that operating hypothesis to an elevated level: showing how to systemize and operationalize human capital decisions, grounded in fact-based data about the immense impact that talent has in achieving a company's goals."

—STEVEN A. DENNING, Chairman Emeritus, General Atlantic

"Attracting and retaining high-performers is as critical to a company's success as building the right product—and likely even more so. *Talent* is an incredible guide for anyone looking to apply a proven, data driven approach to identifying, hiring, and investing in the right people and setting them up for success."

—PEGGY JOHNSON, CEO, Magic Leap

"People management is one of the biggest drivers of success yet it's often the hardest challenge for a CEO to manage. This book provides insights on talent management that will make a difference for any executive!"

—JACKIE RESES, CEO, Post House Capital, ex-CHRO of Square and Yahoo

"Anish Batlaw and Ram Charan make a compelling case that the best human talent is the engine for turning enterprise strategy into operating reality. From graphic studies of a half dozen companies, they show you how to appraise, recruit, and manage that talent. Enterprise leadership is a market-value multiplier, and here is how to secure and support it."

—MICHAEL USEEM, Professor of Management at the Wharton School of the University of Pennsylvania, and author, *The Edge: How 10 CEOs Learned to Lead*

"The importance of human capital cannot be overstated. Anish and Ram make crystal clear why cultivating and retaining strong teams must be high on the list of priorities for any company with serious growth ambitions."

—WILLIAM E. FORD, Chairman & CEO, General Atlantic

"Wow!!! Anish and Ram have not only identified, but captured how to increase market cap through talent. Human capability is the new frontier of market value and their ideas, stories, and tools will be critical for any organization and leader committed to increasing stakeholder value."

—DAVE ULRICH, Rensis Likert Professor, Ross School of Business, University of Michigan Partner, The RBL Group

"There is a science of putting together a leader and a leadership team that delivers to all stakeholders of an enterprise for the long term. In my 30 plus year career I have always believed that every leaders' primary role is to systematically build such a team. Charan and Batlaw lay this out brilliantly in a learnable way, and every practicing leader can use it to create long term value."

—TIGER TYAGARAJAN, President and CEO, Genpact

"Everyone talks about getting the right talent, but few really invest in developing a talent strategy with the intentionality and focus that we do with other critical business levers. In *Talent*, Batlaw and Charan shine a light on best-in-class, real business cases of how talent strategy, when designed and executed properly, changes the game. More importantly, they quantify the direct impact talent selection can have on an organization's overall financial results."

—**JOHNNY C. TAYLOR, JR.**, President & CEO, SHRM (Society for Human Resource Management)

"A must-read for CEOs, CHROs and any C-Suite executive looking to multiply their market value by focusing on their 'bank of talent'. Batlaw and Charan quantifies that value through real-world cases studies and a methodology for how to make talent a value multiplier for any organization."

—**CAROL SURFACE**, Ph.D., CHRO, Medtronic

"In their latest collaboration, *Talent: The Market Cap Multiplier*, Charan and Batlaw perfectly frame the business case, methodology and by highlighting key principles of General Atlantic's Talent Playbook animate how leadership talent and human capital is the one variable...if you get it right...that compresses time to value creation to create enduring, sustainable businesses."

—**KENNY DIPIETRO**, CHRO, Cerevel Therapeutics

TALENT

TALENT

THE MARKET CAP MULTIPLIER

ANISH BATLAW

RAM CHARAN

IDEAPRESS
PUBLISHING

WASHINGTON, D.C.

IDEAPRESS
PUBLISHING

Printed in the United States.

Ideapress Publishing | www.ideapresspublishing.com

Cover Design: Pete Garceau
Interior Design: Jessica Angerstein

Cataloging-in-Publication Data is on file with the Library of Congress.

ISBN: 978-1-64687-077-6

Special Sales
Ideapress Books are available at a special discount for bulk purchases for sales promotions and premiums, or for use in corporate training programs. Special editions, including personalized covers, a custom foreword, corporate imprints, and bonus content, are also available.

From Anish

Dedicated to my Mom and Dad – Lalita and Narendra.

From Ram

Dedicated to the hearts and souls of the joint family
of twelve siblings and cousins living under
one roof for fifty years, whose personal sacrifices made
my formal education possible.

CONTENTS

HIGH PERFORMING TALENT IS THE MARKET CAP MULTIPLIER

RAM CHARAN

I have known Anish Batlaw for twenty-five years, from his days as a Senior Human Resources Executive at PepsiCo and Novartis and then when he was managing talent in the portfolio companies at TPG. I have always been deeply impressed at his trailblazing embrace of a major insight—that the job of identifying and nurturing high-performing executive talent should not be a peripheral corporate function in a silo, outside of the core leadership structure, but a critical partner in creating business success. This may sound like a mere technical idea, moving around some boxes on an organizational chart, but I have learned from my dealings with scores of leading corporations that it is a powerful innovation based on an even-more-powerful insight. Year after year, Anish has enhanced his enviable record of success by identifying, recruiting, and supporting the human capital that is the essential engine of value creation. He shares with me an understanding, borne out by years of experience, that agile, collaborative talent comes before strategy in the restless drama of business success.

One night not long ago, Anish and I had an informal dinner, and I asked one of Jack Welch's favorite questions: "So, what's new, Anish?" For Jack, this wasn't small talk, but an effort to peer into the cutting edge of management systems and hear about new techniques and perspectives. Anish understood and offered a fascinating explanation of how he was innovating the development of talent for General Atlantic, the respected private equity firm, and supporting its portfolio companies with his disciplined approach. He had refined a methodology, he said, that was significantly faster than the usual search process, as well as more systematic. His batting average in getting high performers in the right jobs quickly had soared above the norm. The strong investment returns his firm was realizing were reinforcing the value of his methodology. I was intrigued and we began sharing ideas.

What particularly struck me was the key metric he used in talking about portfolio companies. For many years, investors and many private equity firms focused on EBITDA—cash flow—as a priority, in part because many analysts and institutional investors had a single-minded focus on this measure. But in our conversation, Anish spoke of market value, and of the ways he worked to multiply that value, as his key metric. It was a seemingly simple but important perspective, and it got my attention.

Private equity firms measure performance by looking at internal rate of return and multiple of invested capital for their investors, with the top-tier firms targeting a multiple of about 2.5×, and at times realizing north of 4× over five or six years. Public companies often measure short-term shareholder return (e.g., one to three years). Companies can learn from top-tier private equity firms to focus on value creation over the longer term. Talent is an essential component of this.

Anish described one company in the General Atlantic portfolio and expressed enthusiasm about its leadership and the prospects for scaling up the business rapidly and delivering a better-than-4×-increase in shareholder value in the range of four to five years. What struck me as unusual was the rigorous process he followed for analyzing and developing a talent strategy for portfolio companies. He has a data-driven playbook that is integrated with the deal objectives that General Atlantic has for its investments.

He described how he was working closely with his General Atlantic partners as well as the portfolio company's leadership team to streamline and improve the organizational structure and operating rhythm to scale businesses. He was deploying a precise, proven methodology for getting high-performing talent in the right places at the right time. He was thinking like an entrepreneur, an owner, and holding himself accountable not for checking boxes but for delivering multiples in value.

To put it simply, he was exploding the old, limited vision of what a CHRO does and transforming it into an essential driver in the value creation process. He brought a fresh perspective to a philosophy I have espoused for years, that only the most innovative, nimble, data-focused executives can make speedy decisions in real time in response to rapidly shifting market conditions and seize, or create, the best opportunities. My books have frequently been written with practitioners, so that I can highlight their real-world experiences and explain the principles and lessons behind their work. As Anish explained his own methodology in disrupting the normal CHRO role and reinventing the C-suite operating manual, I realized that there was an important book to be written illuminating that vision and conveying the methods in a way that would benefit other high-performing executives eager to understand the process of value creation.

The coronavirus pandemic hit suddenly, unexpectedly, and tragically in early 2020. The economic disruption has been global and unprecedented in modern times, upsetting numerous tried-and-true principles of corporate behavior. But the shutdown has demonstrated even more clearly the critical role of forward-looking, data-driven leaders and the urgency of deploying the methodology that Anish and I describe in this book. Getting exceptional human capital in place in the best-performing organizational structures is perhaps the best way to navigate this economic crisis and seize the opportunities hidden amid the ruins. It is, ultimately, an extremely optimistic model, because it is about growth, about exciting management teams, about inspiring innovation. Talent is the value creator. Every leader depends on it. It affects business opportunities, business models, strategies, customer acquisition, and strategic execution. That is what's new and what's different in what we describe here.

Who are the exceptional practitioners? How do they deliver such impact? Is their model replicable? This book explains a methodology and practice that can unlock outsized shareholder gains, in many cases in excess of 4× over four to six years. We lay out the methods by analyzing six real-world case studies, drawing out the critical lessons, challenges, near misses, and results that every leader needs to understand.

The companies presented within the case studies represent a high degree of diversity. Some companies are based in the United States, two in the UK, one in Sweden, and one in India. Some have operations internationally across borders, and some are domestic only. Some companies are led by female CEOs, and some are led by male CEOs. Some are hyper growth, one is a turnaround, and one just completed a merger. Some companies are small-cap, some are mid-cap, and one is a large-cap. Irrespective of the situation, each company deploys a talent playbook to compress time-to-value creation.

This book and its timely analysis continue my fifty-year career of advising major corporations, their Boards, CEOs, CHROs, and middle management. As part of that, I have identified practitioners who make a real difference, not once or twice, but consistently and continually, because of their superior insights and the innovative practices and skills I help them develop.

Our six case studies place you in the room, inside the process and the daily drama, and, importantly, inside Anish's thinking. You will see how he diagnoses the problems, with his team and his partners, and devises the solutions. You will observe as Anish and his team conduct interviews, gather data meticulously, take 200 and more pages of notes, and maintain scorecards to ensure that evaluations are as objective and systematic as possible.

That is how his methodology parts way with old practices, gut instinct, and speculation, and drills down into operational reality, uncovering the impediments to the delivery of strong returns and what needs to change to get there. His process is uncommon, but it can be learned. Traditionally, of course, HR has not played such a core role in most corporations. It has existed in a silo. Rarely has the CHRO had a sense of ownership or been held accountable for enhancing overall business performance. That accountability is key to the innovative process Anish has developed and employed.

Explained in detail, with nuance and a sense of the challenges of real-world situations, this methodology is replicable. It is exponentially better than the previous, fragmented approaches of the traditional HR officer. These are some of the fundamental lessons we will extract from these case studies.

The case of Oak Street Health, an exceptional hypergrowth company building a national chain of clinics for treating Medicare patients, shows how young and extremely talented CEO/founders can benefit from careful development and leadership support to help them build the right team and, in the process, prepare for the rigors of operating a complex company that is multiplying in size, and value, as it expands across the country.

The story of Vishal Retail, a pioneering hypermarket chain in India, tracks how a company, on the verge of collapse at the time of the investment, was put on a path of enormous growth and success by hiring not just an excellent CEO, but by surrounding him with a high-performing leadership team. Anish also provided mentoring and smart support on the Board. It was a remarkable rebuilding operation led by exhaustively researched talent upgrades.

Depop is an exciting e-commerce disrupter that had performed superbly in its home market, the UK, but needed to upgrade significantly if it was to meet its objective of taking its fast-fashion resale app global, and especially to compete successfully in the US. A highly skilled CEO was evaluated carefully and given support in rebuilding her leadership team, upgrading several key roles, and improving her communication with her team to launch a reorganization that could manage these challenges.

Argus Media is a highly promising commodity price and energy market intelligence company that faced turmoil at the time of the investment because of a clash between the CEO and the Chair. That can happen, of course, in the real world, and Chief Talent Officers must learn how to navigate the situations with a cautious, objective, data-driven approach to ensure that the right management is put in place—not to resolve today's problems, but to have the ability to drive the business to where it needs to be in three to five years. The ultimate decision on which of those executives would stay and which needed to go required staying rooted in the need to select the leader who had the ability to create long-term value, which paid off handsomely.

In the case of Hemnet, Sweden's dominant online site for real estate listings, the case demonstrates the care needed to evaluate a sitting CEO at the time of the investment. Anish needed to determine quickly if the chair at the time was the right person to scale the company up going forward and, if not, how they would select a high-performing, tech-savvy replacement in a relatively small market. The case also shows the essential role for supporting a new CEO, evaluating the organizational structure and the operating rhythm of the leadership team, and providing guidance on how to optimize the business for withstanding the stresses of scaling.

The most important lesson from all the cases we analyze is that applying this talent methodology has proven, repeatedly, to be a reliable value creator. I have cross-checked these cases to ensure that we correctly assess the methods and describe the results. We explain how understanding and implementing these innovative approaches to talent management can support faster decision-making and farsighted thinking from the CEOs and leadership teams and can chart creative strategies. This is about discipline, analysis, performance, and that exponential increase in value. This is about disrupting and rethinking the role of talent and leadership in the organization.

In Anish's hands, C-suite planning and execution have been transformed. In my long career as a consultant to CEOs and Boards, I have often advised top corporations on the primacy of talent issues, and some of the thirty-one books I have written have described my own long-standing embrace of the indisputable, and sometimes underappreciated, role that human capital plays in delivering value. If you get that right, everything else follows.

But there is a related lesson. This model is not solely for private equity firms or even venture capital start-ups. Those businesses may have the flexibility to embrace these insights quickly, but even some venerable, extremely large corporations have demonstrated that a savvy focus on grooming high-performing talent and giving it the support to grow can create surprising multiples in value. That is what we show in our chapter on Johnson & Johnson.

You, the reader, are likely a CEO or restless C-suite innovator, and you share this commitment to delivering higher market value. That is a strength. This book will help you get there.

CHAPTER 1

TALENT: THE ENGINE OF VALUE CREATION

WILLIAM E. FORD, CHAIRMAN
AND CEO, GENERAL ATLANTIC

General Atlantic has enjoyed a long history of success as a pioneering growth equity investor by applying a distinctive formula, enabling the firm to create exceptional multiples in value by building up great companies. The firm was founded by the entrepreneur and philanthropist Chuck Feeney, who had previously cofounded the airport retailer Duty Free Shoppers. In 1980, he established General Atlantic as a direct investment entity to support visionary founders, as well as magnify his ability to "give back" and achieve his mission to give away his accumulated wealth in his lifetime.

In 1982, Chuck formally established Atlantic Philanthropies. The Foundation operated anonymously for its first fifteen years because of Chuck's desire for flexibility and a low profile. In its thirty-eight years of existence, Atlantic Philanthropies provided close to $10 billion in grants, creating opportunity and promoting greater fairness and equity in communities around the world. Chuck has said before, "I see little reason to delay giving when so much good can be achieved through supporting worthwhile causes today." This is the guiding principle of the "Giving While Living" philosophy that has become an inspiration to so many philanthropists and still permeates the culture at GA today.

The founding team at General Atlantic, including Steve Denning, former CEO and Chairman Emeritus, and Dave Hodgson, Vice Chairman, believed deeply in the power of technology and its ubiquitous potential. Our firm's strength is partnering with high-performing entrepreneurs and leadership teams and scaling up promising global businesses, investing in innovative products, new markets, and, importantly, people. It is a uniquely optimistic philosophy, a commitment to creating durable business successes that enrich their numerous stakeholders, customers, employees and executives, communities, and investors.

Even with GA's strong track record, Bill Ford, our CEO since 2007, reflected on that formula a few years ago and felt we could do even better. His objectives focused on what his long experience in the industry told him was one of the most elusive yet consequential—and in many ways underappreciated—elements in the success of GA's portfolio businesses: talent.

Bill believed that, in many instances, it was taking too long to install the right leadership teams at portfolio companies, or that the companies were having to change leadership multiple times before finding the right fit, costing them valuable time and diminishing returns. The data clearly supported his views. The solution, Bill decided, was to invest in building a comprehensive, data-driven, and disciplined approach to identifying, assessing, and nurturing high-performing talent and building high-performing cultures in a consistent way. His fundamental insight, borne out by an analysis of our performance over the years, was that talent was the key engine of value creation, particularly in today's challenging, and rapidly changing, knowledge economy. Getting the right leaders in place quickly and more consistently needed to become a core discipline for the firm.

"I had a deep conviction, particularly with growth companies, that talent was the single most significant variable in differentiating outstanding performance from just good success," Bill said in an interview. "Before, we focused on having the right investment, the right price and deal structure. But we've learned talent is as important as all of those things." By his own account, Bill has become something of an evangelist for talent and has taken a series of concrete steps that have been transformative for the firm and its portfolio.

Today, GA's talent function is integral to the investment process, deeply involved in portfolio management, and a critical part of value creation. My role, as an Operating Partner within the firm, is focused entirely on supporting our portfolio companies in building high-quality management teams and Boards of Directors, and in developing highly engaged and diverse workforces. This work is made possible because of Bill's sponsorship.

Like Bill, I have been a student of leadership for my entire career and have witnessed firsthand the impact that talent has on creation of value. I have worked in the private equity industry for over fourteen years, which includes seven years with GA and six years previously with TPG Capital. Before coming into private equity, I worked at PepsiCo, Microsoft, and Novartis, where I came to understand the universal impact that strategic talent management has on companies across different industries, geographies, and stages of scale.

Within a few months of my joining GA, Bill and I set a long-term goal of "getting the right management team in place at portfolio companies within six months of closing a deal". That was a critical first step and, importantly, it became a firm-wide goal that I share with my partners on the investment side. I then worked with Bill and our partners to codify the approach in a landmark series of memos in 2016. This model, which we call the Talent Playbook, is built on a foundation of rigorous analysis of data, a consistent methodology, and replicable results.

"Building leadership capability within our portfolio companies is one of the most important things we do," Bill once wrote.

To develop this playbook, we started by looking at data on our investments over a period of twelve years. The findings were striking. We found that when we made a mistake with a CEO change, the average IRR for those deals dropped by about 82 percent compared to when we got the CEO change right the first time. In addition, when a change was successfully executed within the first year of the deal, the average IRR ended up being 6× greater than if the change was made after the first year. Backing the right leader and teams and moving with speed and conviction lead to exceptional results; getting it wrong can be damaging.

All deals that are presented to the Investment Committee include a page dedicated to talent and culture. This page typically includes an overview of current management capability and future needs, Board composition, and observations on culture and diversity. Not only do we look at the top one or two executives at each company, but we go deep within each organization to gain an understanding of their entire leadership team, organization structure, operating rhythm, talent systems and employee engagement.

On the heels of a deal, we immerse ourselves with the management team to better understand areas of strength and potential opportunities for development, all in the context of scaling the business. We then synthesize our findings and help the CEO develop and execute a talent and organization strategy aligned with the deal thesis. This has become a core process for GA.

One of the most challenging variables in our talent methodology is identifying executives who have the ability to build and manage the business for far bigger and more complex than its current dimensions. Perhaps the most difficult aspect of this part of the process is being willing to part ways with leaders who may be performing well, who may be loyal and well-liked, but who are considered to not have the necessary skills and leadership to take the business through the next stage of its journey.

Growth CEOs often "instinctively know they have people on the team who have been successful in the first chapter but who aren't equipped to support the company through its next phase of growth," Bill said. "It's the hardest part, especially when those same individuals were by your side and instrumental in getting you through the challenging early years of starting a business. They are often loyal, hardworking, and capable, but if they are not equipped for the next phase, you have to act in the best interest of the company and elevate the team to set the company up for success."

"Even as a Board Director, it's an uncomfortable feeling to watch this happen," Bill continued. "But these leaders placed the mission of the company and where they wanted to take the business above that loyalty. It's a hard decision. However, if you don't make those changes, you will start to stunt your growth."

He added, "The great growth CEOs are willing to make changes to the organization even while they're going 50 to 60 miles an hour, and make very difficult decisions about talent."

Ultimately, Bill emphasized, the greatest strength he seeks in a growth leader is not just having a farsighted vision and a strategy for obtaining it, but also having the ability to build an exceptional team equipped to manage increased scale and complexity and drive execution.

"The great ones are leaders, not managers, in the sense that leaders take people to places they can't even imagine are possible. Managers effectively manage resources and advance a company in a very positive way. True leaders don't have irrational goals—they're rational, even when they seem unattainable."

Another key initiative to advance our talent agenda was building a database of proven, high-performing executives that we know and can turn to when needs arise across the portfolio. We call it our Talent Bank. Our function follows a disciplined process for seeking out talented executives in the marketplace, inviting them to engage with us in conversations on their backgrounds and goals even before there is a need in the portfolio. Our partners actively contribute to the Talent Bank.

Maintaining the Talent Bank is time-consuming and challenging—we track over 4,000 executives—but the payoff is significant. We have found that working with a search firm for a key senior hire typically takes from 150 to 160 days. When we can turn to our network through the Talent Bank and other avenues, we can make a key hire in as few as ten days, having already been well-acquainted with the candidates. This strategy has also allowed us to build a pipeline of diverse leaders and has contributed to a 50 percent increase in female executive hires across the portfolio from 2018 to 2020. We have also been able to help our Boards add diverse talent. As of the end of Q2 2021, 52 percent of Independent Directors on our US Boards were diverse.

The impact of this engine is proving dramatic, especially in a highly competitive talent market. After launching the Talent Bank in 2015, we sourced 30 percent of placements across the portfolio from our network just three years later. In the first quarter of 2021 alone, 62 percent of hires came from our Talent Bank. Additionally, the time required to hire CXO and Board Directors has dropped from 162 days on average in 2014 to fewer than eighty days on average in the first quarter of 2021.

"We needed an accelerant to our process, and the Talent Bank is the accelerant," Bill said in our interview. "It changed the game, and it's become a real competitive advantage for the firm."

Our partners have bought into the process. "What Anish has done is to create a lot of believers among the Managing Director group," Bill said. "Before they might have said, 'Look, the hard part is finding the investment and paying the right price, structuring it right, getting to an exit.' But I think we've elevated talent to be just as important as those things. And I think it's the most important part of the added value that we bring to the companies."

GA is itself also a growth company, like the companies we invest in. Under Bill's leadership, the firm has grown enormously—assets under management have increased from $12 billion in 2007 to more than $65 billion in 2021. He further expanded our international presence by opening offices in Jakarta, Singapore, Beijing, Shanghai, and Mexico City as our perspectives and interests have widened. As Bill emphasizes, this is all part of a broader goal of leaving the firm better than he found it and making sure it is prepared to perform even better under its next leaders.

"The central focus of my job is to ensure that I do whatever I can to make my Managing Directors successful," Bill said. "The firm is larger than any one individual. When it was handed to me, my job was to make it better and stronger, and then hand it on to someone else. I think about succession all the time."

Importantly, Bill has adjusted his management strategies to deal with the stresses that can accompany rapid growth. He has taken the bold step of applying the same fundamentals of our Talent Playbook to change the way we evaluate, develop, and support our own partners at GA. Under Bill's leadership, GA has learned to better develop talent from within, as well as effectively hire senior talent from the outside.

"We are fortunate to have a track record of bringing in people like Anish, acculturating them and making them successful on our platform," said Bill. "We are unique in our ability to do that. Now, I'd still say that 60 percent of our management committee or leadership team is homegrown, but 40 percent is from the outside."

Behind this observation is a fundamental truth about GA's philosophy. "We welcome disruption and see change as an empowering ally," Bill said.

On the firm's fortieth anniversary, Bill wrote: "For the past four decades, this firm has been steadfast as a partner to entrepreneurs in helping them build businesses that can change the world. Our values will continue to guide the decisions we make: a global mindset and growth orientation, with a focus on innovation and creativity. We remain committed to supporting our firm, portfolio companies, capital partners, and society more broadly: to keep striving, progressing, and tackling the challenges ahead together, for the next forty years and beyond."

CHAPTER 2

HOW A HIGH-POTENTIAL CEO ACHIEVED 75× REVENUE GROWTH

OAK STREET HEALTH

I showed up early for a meeting at General Atlantic's offices in Greenwich, Connecticut, one morning in 2015. I was new, having started at General Atlantic just a few months before, so I was used to seeing unfamiliar faces in the offices. I was the first to arrive at our conference room, but a young man in his early thirties soon walked in and introduced himself. It was Mike Pykosz, the CEO of Oak Street Health, a start-up focused on Medicare patients, with an enormously ambitious plan for rapid growth and wraparound care. He and another cofounder of the company, Geoff Price, the Chief Operating Officer, were there to discuss a potential investment.

Mike and I shook hands, then poured ourselves some coffee and began to chat. Mike quickly got serious and said he was delighted that General Atlantic had included me in this meeting, though I was a senior executive involved in talent strategy and leadership and not, strictly speaking, a deal guy. "I want to work with you," he said, and explained that a vital priority was to build out the company's executive team and its clinics with talent, and provide the right leadership and incentives. This was essential to realizing Oak Street's promise of providing superior value to investors and excellent medical outcomes for its elderly patients. He said he knew he needed professional support in this critical strategic goal and was eager for my advice.

For me, it was a telling introduction both to Mike and to Oak Street. The three founders were clearly bright and capable, and they had been operating their new venture for more than two years with some favorable results. But, as I would soon learn, their background was in consulting rather than ground-level operations. They had all come from the Boston Consulting Group, so they had some good business experience, but not much in actually managing people or a company, particularly one in as complex an industry as healthcare for seniors. I wanted to better understand what they needed to fulfill their plans.

General Atlantic's dealmakers had met the founders previously and some of our investment experts were following Oak Street's early progress. The three entrepreneurs had set up Oak Street Health in 2012, opened their first clinic for seniors on Chicago's North Side in 2013, and had some discussions with General Atlantic the next year. The Oak Street group understood the healthcare space well and recognized the prospects for rapid expansion if they could scale the business properly. The team and its data-driven plan excited the investment partner looking at the company, Robbert Vorhoff, who has exceptional knowledge and experience in the healthcare field. Robb had been exploring and analyzing how the Affordable Care Act was creating large opportunities in the healthcare market, and he was seeking promising investments.

Healthcare companies often focus on the payer space or the care provider space, but not both. Oak Street was creating an innovative company that included improvements to both sides of the system, and was sharply improving patient satisfaction and outcomes. Oak Street planned to build a national chain of primary-care clinics for elderly patients enrolled in Medicare, and many who were dual enrolled in Medicaid. This is a challenging, often underserved population that generally has very low incomes and numerous health conditions, many of them chronic. Many in that group have also had inadequate health care for years.

Oak Street's model provides thorough, excellent preventive care, easy access, and reliable treatment of chronic conditions, thus reducing the number and length of hospital stays and improving outcomes for what is a large, rapidly growing senior population. By seeking to align the interests of the medical care provider, payers, and the patients themselves, the company's strategy also delivered on an important, if long-neglected, social purpose and has greatly enriched the lives of many people.

Delivering on this deal thesis would be tough, but the founders were no ordinary team. Robb described them as three "A players." They had known one another for some time, had worked together, and had developed a great deal of trust and respect for one another, which helped meld them into an effective team that multiplied their capabilities. They were all Harvard graduates—Mike from the law school, Geoff from the business school, and Griffin completed his residency at the medical school. They were analytical, deeply understood their market, and were clear about their need to learn how to manage this complex business effectively. Even so, the company's plans for rapid, national expansion were interesting but still unproven. That was the initial question: whether they had the experience to operate their model for the clinics and scale the idea as projected.

Robb recognized that everything ultimately depended on execution, and great precision in that execution. As I listened to the presentation at that meeting in Greenwich, I understood Robb's reasoning that talent would play a vital role in creating value. Their strategy required building and staffing clinics across many states, training the staff to exacting standards, maintaining consistent quality in care, establishing rigorous controls and compliance, monitoring all the procedures, and communicating with the payers—insurance companies. It required staff that was not locked into the medical industry's somewhat conservative operating methods. It required a strong internal culture that motivated the staff under Mike's vision as CEO.

Talent professionals are constantly considering the importance of experience. We ask whether job candidates or sitting executives have enough of it, if they have the right kind, how we can help them develop or deepen it. We try to peer into the future to see whether these leaders have the experience to navigate challenges they may have never encountered before. Our principal concern with Oak Street was gauging its ability to manage the scaling-up process. It meant asking not whether the company had the ability to manage a $13 million company—their revenues at that time—but whether it could handle a $100 million or even $500 million company.

From the beginning, it was clear that Mike did not just want capital from General Atlantic. He wanted support on strategy within the healthcare sector and technology, and advice from me on growing as a leader, helping the company develop a nimble talent base, and helping to design an appropriate incentive system to align everyone behind his vision and be sure they were well-compensated over the longer term for superior performance.

The founders showed a clear command of the data and the dynamics of their market and its risks. They spoke with passion and lucidity about the clinics and the patients they served, the strength of their care model, the evidence supporting their innovations, and the quality controls and discipline needed. They appreciated the challenges of patient acquisition. We learned that the modeled economics of their clinics compared favorably with traditional primary-care providers. But they acknowledged some key unmet objectives: for instance, they still used Excel for some key population health tools and needed to develop digital systems for their own tracking, reporting, and care model processes.

Mike had confidence in the concept of the care the company would provide. His conviction made his story more compelling. By the end of that three-hour meeting in Greenwich, I appreciated both the opportunity to deliver enormous multiples in value and the hurdles. Several points were converging in my mind as I reviewed what I was ascertaining. Mike showed excellent analytical capabilities and a command of the data needed to seize opportunities. He showed a real hunger for information and knowledge and eagerly sought out support for his leadership. He used the metrics from tracking key performance indicators wisely. Initial patient acquisition was positive. And he got an excellent reference from Humana for the quality of the operation and the patient outcomes.

After the meeting, I reflected on our conversation and whether I believed we could back Mike as the CEO. Given his limited operating experience, we would be betting on his potential and his ability to mature as a leader. As part of this process, I collected my thoughts on Mike's dominant strengths as well as the areas where we would have to take a chance, synthesizing the data points and asking myself whether the executive had shown the capacity for scaling up with the business—in this case, an operationally intensive and complex organization. It was important that we clearly understand the precise nature of the risk we might be taking on so we could mitigate it if necessary.

After working through this exercise, I shared my evaluation with Robb, summarized below, suggesting that I believed Mike could successfully scale up as projected.

Track Record: Although Mike was early in his career as an operator, he did have a track record of delivering against early projections, which we identified through multiple rounds of dialogue with the business. Additionally, Mike and his cofounders had all excelled when they were at the Boston Consulting Group and demonstrated progression during the first chapters of their careers.

Strategic Thinking: I scored Mike high on his strategic thinking, clarity, and ability to examine issues from multiple angles. He's competitive, eager to find ways of differentiating the company, analytical, and well-versed in his market. But he seemed to have much to learn about the retailing and marketing dimension of his model, which directly affected patient acquisition.

Learning Agility: I applauded his self-awareness and self-critical attitude and noted that his passion should push his eagerness to learn and grow. Mike openly acknowledged that he needed support, exhibiting a quality that most top-performing CEOs have.

Drive for Results: I noted that Mike is ambitious and has a strong orientation toward achievement, will set challenging goals, and will push his team to stretch, while setting a strong example on what success takes. He also focuses on data and metrics for rigorously tracking business performance.

Team Leadership: Mike was going through a steep learning curve, but he was aware of the importance of attracting high-quality talent into the company. As the business scaled up, he would be challenged on how to empower his team and facilitate shared solutions. He would also be tested on his ability to manage change, take it through the social architecture of a bigger and growing organization, and get it executed on the ground. Bringing on executives with deep operating experience would reduce the risk.

Interpersonal Influence: I found that Mike listens well, can build rapport with a broad range of people, communicates effectively, and can use those skills, plus his understanding of the business, to find influence points and establish partnerships.

I concluded that, overall, Mike and Geoff undoubtedly brought strong strategic and commercial acumen to Oak Street, but that they needed operating leaders who could work as a team and complement one another to deliver on the deal thesis. Mike recognized this. Having grown up loving basketball, he liked to say that he learned from the sport how important a strong team mentality and complementary skills were to winning. His trust in his team was reflected in the way he treats his two other cofounders as equals.

What we observed and would learn further as I worked with Mike was his ability to reflect, to question his ideas, and to consider alternatives rather than remain locked in to one operating pattern. He had an understanding that, as a leader, he had to constantly find a balance between being rigidly logical and data-driven and embracing a more empathetic approach to his role, relying at times on articulating a strong narrative to convince people to follow his vision. At that time, the company had revenues of about $13 million and had raised capital from some other private equity firms as well as a group of "angels," other healthcare veterans with capital to invest. General Atlantic took an influential minority stake in December 2015.

It was a promising start, but, as can happen in the investment world, we quickly hit a bump. Only months after our investment, Oak Street reported to us that it had fallen short of its patient enrollment projections. It was a jolt. Enrollment was the revenue driver, and the shortfall raised potential questions about their model and potentially undercut their financial forecast. This was their first reporting period after our investment, accentuating the concern. Had they misjudged the market? Had their execution been weak?

Robb asked Mike to analyze the problem, assess what went wrong, and develop a path forward. Mike promptly went to work, again demonstrating the intellectual horsepower behind the Oak Street team. He gathered data and addressed the issues he found. Robb had placed a lot of trust in the young CEO at a moment when others might have resorted to finger-pointing. That trust, Mike says, engendered a new level of loyalty and commitment, which gave him powerful motivation to justify the trust with better performance.

Enrollment eventually picked up and Oak Street implemented its programs for treating the complex needs of the patients. For instance, about 40 percent are dual-eligible for Medicare and Medicaid and have an average income of less than $21,000 a year. As expected, the vast majority are over sixty-five. Over 80 percent have two or more chronic conditions, such as hypertension, diabetes, congestive heart failure, or chronic obstructive pulmonary disease, and they take an average of 7.2 medications.

Ultimately, Oak Street's success relied heavily on its clinical care model and delivering better outcomes at a lower cost. A key area of focus for all three cofounders was ensuring that they were constantly assessing and improving their care model to result in better outcomes for patients. They established standardized care protocols, which were disseminated to the clinics and practitioners and created a culture centered on delivering the best care. This also required a strong training program for the clinical staff as well as the recruitment and retention of top performers.

Oak Street initially ran the clinics on a fee-for-service basis, but later transitioned to a risk-based model in which the multiple insurers they work with pay them a flat fee for most patients, giving them the opportunity to profit by keeping costs low. But they also face the risk of losses if treatment costs exceed expectations and if outcomes miss targets because of poor or inadequate care. That gives Oak Street incentives to deliver consistent, high-quality preventive care, easy access, and quick, responsive treatment, limiting emergencies and improving overall health for a population that is often underserved. The model is a major boon to a healthcare system under great stress and filled with inequality. That positive sense of purpose pervades Oak Street's culture.

Among their milestones, Oak Street Health has cut hospital admissions for its patients in half and reduced emergency room visits by half. It has cut thirty-day readmission rates after hospital stays by 35 percent. In the process, it has built an outstanding patient experience with a 90 percent Net Promoter Score.

To succeed, the parts of Oak Street's business had to be synchronized for coordinated functioning, with excellent monitoring and record keeping and the application of sophisticated technology. And on top of that, this had to be done as Oak Street was expanding, adding clinics, hiring and training new staff, and adding to the strain on middle management and senior executives. Applying sophisticated technology was one key to reaching all these goals. Mike recognized this as we helped him hire a high-quality CIO to strengthen their technology.

Everything depended on precise execution of a complex, multifaceted plan; effective execution depended on experienced operational management. It had to be replicable over dozens of clinics spread out over many states. Problems and failures, which were inevitable, had to be addressed promptly and flexibly, always a management challenge. With a company growing this fast and this consistently, decisions had a compounding effect on the business. The company's growth is complex, requiring extensive background work in selecting sites for new clinics, hiring new staff, providing training, and instilling the cost discipline. Oak Street has developed effectively, maintaining quality control and compliance. When all those elements are working in coordination and synchronized, the increase in enterprise value can be exceedingly rapid; it is also true, however, that missteps or poor execution can compound negatively just as rapidly. This is where Geoff, Oak Street's COO, played an integral role.

The proper response to these challenges was to build a sound platform to allow the business to scale. We were comfortable that this might, at times, temper short-term growth. Expectations were less likely to race ahead of performance that way, and the growth would be more sustainable. As a result, the growth they enjoy is more consistent and predictable. And, because the operations tend to be functioning smoothly, performance targets are met consistently, and the value multiplies more rapidly.

We also recommended that they develop a high-quality executive team around the CEO and his cofounders. A great CEO establishes high standards for the leadership team and builds the team in the context of not where the company is today, but where it will be in the future. Over time, Mike knew he needed to bring in a new CFO, General Counsel, and head of Human Resources. With our support, and relying in part on our Talent Bank, we were able to attract three high-quality leaders of these functions that continue to help the business scale.

One of the most critical areas where we provided support was in developing an effective incentive plan. When a private equity firm is an investor, executive compensation and incentives are indispensable to assure that corporate leadership is aligned with the key longer-term investment objectives and is rewarded for delivering the return on investment that the deal was premised on.

The company from Day One relied less on annual cash compensation (i.e., salary plus bonuses) and more on long-term equity grants that would vest over a period of years and be subject to performance. My colleague Alex Stahl and I worked with Oak Street to adapt an early equity plan to a structure that would allow for the company to continue to leverage equity compensation as it scaled, so that the value of that equity was many multiples of a participant's cash compensation and tied to a percentage of the increase in value realized by the deal. That potential payoff motivates executives to work not just for annual or quarterly targets, but with an eye on longer-term value creation. This gets everyone thinking like an owner, and it is part of the value proposition that private equity investors offer executives in portfolio companies because it encourages value creation for all stakeholders.

Our equity plans are tied to increasing the business's value over a period of perhaps three to five years, relying on taking, for instance, a $100 million revenue company to $500 million, or to $1 billion. These plans are geared toward performance, with more of the equity vesting for achieving a higher multiple on the original investment value. Under this system, a senior executive could see equity realization that is greater than 10x their cash compensation. In addition, General Atlantic will, at times, permit the leaders to invest their own capital in the deal, another opportunity to deliver a reward that gives executives skin in the game and increased alignment of goals. This really allows a company to hire mission-critical talent ahead of the curve.

Mike embraced this general approach, but finding a good balance was a challenge, and he relied on us to help him fine-tune their systems. It was especially important in the early stages of the deal to attract the right talent ahead of the curve while keeping salaries and bonuses low enough to not burn through the company's cash. Recruiting high-quality leaders often required them to take below 50th percentile cash compensation in exchange for the upside in equity. It was critical to have clear communication and education around the equity plan and to get people to understand and buy into Oak Street's growth story, so that they understood the potential value of their packages. Mike's perspective was that if someone were not willing to make that trade-off, then they were likely not the right person for the company.

Mike confronted the difficulty of striking this balance after Oak Street established itself and was operating efficiently. Some senior staff who had accepted below-median salaries at the time of hire in exchange for potentially more profitable, longer-term equity grants decided to leave. Some were eager to cash out and realize the gain in value or to hang on to their equity even though they were no longer Oak Street employees. But the equity grants came with vesting requirements, and when some of those who wanted to leave realized they would lose their unvested equity, it created emotional confrontations, particularly for those who felt they had sacrificed. Mike and I discussed this at some length and agreed that he should stay true to the principles behind the program.

Also unique to our compensation philosophy is that our total compensation packages are top of market for the most critical roles. Most compensation philosophies are set to offer market median compensation across the board for employees, likely attracting median or average talent. Our belief is that top performers in critical roles can drive value creation that is multiples above an average performer, so we are willing to stretch when required. We benchmark equity compensation ahead of the curve based on our expectations of where the company will be in the future. Mike has bought into this philosophy as well, and consistently rewards Oak Street's top performers. We helped develop an equity "refresh" program that rewarded high performers with additional equity annually, further retaining top talent. Oak Street was able to attract and retain a fantastic team. The team built an impactful and valuable company; in turn, team members shared in the value creation.

In addition, we discussed the best way of determining annual cash incentives (bonuses). Again, the issue was balance. I suggested that he set financial goals that should be achievable for executive bonuses to be paid, but I also urged that they not be too far a stretch. Establishing a bonus pool that nobody can access is not a success and can have an adverse, demotivating effect on employees. The goals needed to be realistic, and Mike needed to be confident in the company's ability to reach them. I encouraged him to simplify the plan to focus on a few key drivers of the business. We discussed providing upside in the bonus pool for outperformance and giving more significant bonuses to top performers. This would provide the shorter-term motivation that is important to retaining key personnel, and, in the longer term, attracts and supports executives who believe they can bend the performance curve upward.

A strong, balanced incentive program is also a good defense against executive poaching by other companies.

Another key issue was building the right middle management for the company. The point was not just to provide strong capabilities for near-term success, but to ensure that the company had a pipeline of leaders, a critical mass of management and leadership capacity. Scaling up successfully relied heavily on developing that capacity.

While it is potentially more expensive to hire top talent from high-quality business schools or consulting firms, this highly skilled cadre of midlevel managers would create a lot of value if given the opportunity to mature into strong senior-level executives in the future, with appropriate incentives. That would allow Oak Street, over time, to promote from within as senior-level positions opened, and secure high-quality talent immersed in the company's systems and culture. Recruiting and developing high-potential talent became a strategic objective to increase the leadership capacity at Oak Street and to expand its bandwidth for managing rapid growth. For a company scaling up at such a rapid rate, enhancing this leadership capacity is crucial. Oak Street has hired dozens of top-tier MBA students into the leadership program.

As a high-potential CEO, Mike was also focused on developing himself. He and I had multiple conversations about his development and what he could do to accelerate it. We spoke about the long-range perspective he needed to bring to his planning and management and how important it was to keep in mind not where the company was today and the incremental steps it might need to reach its objectives in a year or two, but to flip that perspective. This required regular monitoring and care to make sure he was using his time wisely. A CEO's time is the most precious commodity, and they need to focus their energy on where they would have the most impact. Mike also engaged a coach who could mentor him. He is constantly thinking toward the future of the business and how it will need to evolve to get there.

That focus has delivered exceptional results. Oak Street is well ahead of General Atlantic's expectations, and the multiplying increase in value has made it one of the best investments the firm has ever made. Our patience and constant support have also paid off in another way, as the founders, despite their relative inexperience at the onset of the investment, have grown into great business leaders and should be seen as the benchmark all founders should aspire to.

Oak Street's next chapter was to prepare for life as a public company. When thinking about transitioning from a private to a public company, three talent-related areas should be considered: the management team, the Board of Directors, and compensation. As a public company CEO, Mike would need to spend a significant amount of his time on public company matters. This made it even more important for him to have a strong leadership team that could fill in that vacuum. By strengthening the team ahead of the curve, Mike was set up to seamlessly transition to this role.

Mike, Robb, and the rest of the team also made it an early priority to build a world-class Board to support Oak Street's growth. This included focusing on diversity and independence, and establishing Board committees well before the company would go public. It was critical to think ahead in terms of where the company would be in the future and attract Directors that fit that vision. Years before the IPO, Oak Street appointed Dr. Mohit Kaushal, a former member of President Obama's White House Health IT task force, and Carl Daley, SVP of Retail Strategy and Operations at Humana. Leading up to and through the IPO, they continued to bolster the Board, adding Dr. Regina Benjamin, a former US Surgeon General; Kim Keck, CEO of Blue Cross Blue Shield Association; Cheryl Dorsey, President of Echoing Green; and Julie Klapstein, founding CEO of Availity, a health information network. A majority of the nonexecutive Directors on the Board are diverse.

Lastly, the company focused on ensuring that it could successfully transition its compensation program to one that is in line with public company norms. This included a shift to annual equity awards, a significant departure from the approach discussed earlier in this chapter. As the IPO was projected to unlock significant value creation for the executive team, it became critical to put in place a new incentive program with strong retentive power and ensured that there was continuity on the management team through and post-IPO. We didn't want the team to view the IPO as the finish line. Alex and I analyzed each executive's outstanding equity and developed a framework based on benchmarks, unvested equity, and criticality/performance in role to determine the appropriate new incentives.

In August 2020, the company successfully completed its IPO, and it continues to deliver outstanding returns for its shareholders. Our thesis that Mike had the potential to scale up with the business has proven correct. Not only was Mike able to take Oak Street to $100 million and then $500 million in revenues, but Oak Street now has more than $1 billion in annual revenues and over eighty clinics. In the past five years, the company has created more than $13 billion in value and, even more importantly, has changed the landscape of senior care in the US. It has contributed to a 51 percent reduction in hospital admissions and a 42 percent reduction in the thirty-day readmission rate. There has also been a 51 percent reduction in expensive emergency department visits. This, we are certain, is just the beginning.

KEY LEARNINGS

OAK STREET HEALTH

RAM CHARAN

I am personally connected to this story, as I coached Mike and the team. Oak Street Health is a forward-looking innovator, an excellent investment opportunity, and it surfaces numerous best practices that should be considered when scaling a business.

- The company founders had developed an excellent business model that provided superior care for the country's growing number of Medicare patients. But a core question remained: could the founders deliver on the growth agenda? Robb asked Anish to help him assess the leadership team. Anish uncovered that while Mike and Geoff did not bring extensive operating experience, they were high-potential athletes. With the right investment in their development, they had the ability to drive outsized returns. As the War for Talent intensifies, Boards, CEOs, and CHROs will need to get better at identifying high-potential talent and betting on their success.

- The founders doubled down on potential as they implemented their own program designed to bring in high-caliber talent from top-tier business schools and consulting firms. They had the foresight to understand that if they needed a certain number of strong leaders in critical roles as a $100 million company, they would need a multiple of that as a $500 million or $1 billion company. While costly up front, the program paid off in spades. By providing these individuals with stretch opportunities, Oak Street was able to groom future leaders of their business from within. In an increasingly competitive recruiting environment, having a deep bench of talent that you can draw upon internally can greatly differentiate you from the competition.

- A particularly important element of Anish's work was designing the right incentive programs for the leadership team to propel them forward on the next wave of value creation. This program was unusual in that executives traded cash compensation for equity. Not only did this tightly align the interests of the executives with the interests of the shareholders, giving them the opportunity to increase their total earnings if the business outperformed, but it also had a major impact on retention.

- Also unique to this program was the forward-looking approach that Anish and his team used to benchmark compensation. Instead of benchmarking against other similarly sized companies, they compared Oak Street to companies that were at a larger scale, where Oak Street planned to be in four or five years. This allowed the company to attract talent from larger organizations for the most critical roles. This can be a lesson for all organizations as they develop their talent strategies. Leaders should assess the talent they have and the talent they need in the lens of where the company will be, not where they are today. While this approach is more expensive, CEOs need to view it as an investment in increasing the readiness to scale. CEOs also need to invest in their own development to improve their ability to lead higher-caliber professionals.

CHAPTER 3

PREPARING A DYNAMIC CEO FOR THE NEXT LEVEL OF HYPERGROWTH

DEPOP

Melis Kahya Akar, one of my partners at General Atlantic, stuck her head into my office one day. She was just coming from an Investment Committee meeting where she had introduced the opportunity to invest in a Gen Z-focused, fashion resale marketplace called Depop, and her excitement was palpable. Depop, based in London, was growing at a screaming pace and had fantastic potential for global expansion. This was a best-in-class business. Melis asked if I would spend time with the CEO and support her in developing an effective leadership and organizational development strategy for an aggressive scaling-up process.

Melis understood the company well, how it cleverly disrupted the fast-fashion and peer-to-peer e-commerce sectors by supporting both the buyer and seller sides of its marketplace. She had followed the company for more than a year. Depop's exceptional potential was obvious to her.

Depop launched in 2011 and experienced explosive popularity with one of the most sought-after but elusive consumer groups, Gen Z. Customers were embracing the site not just to buy and sell "pre-loved" clothing, but as a community site where they could express their fashion sensibilities, learn about emerging styles in real time, and toy with becoming trendsetters. With its emphasis on fashion recycling, Depop appeals to an ethos of sustainability and green culture, a big Gen Z draw. How big a draw? One-third of all sixteen- to twenty-four-year-olds in the UK have downloaded the app, and its user retention is best in class.

As Maria Raga, Depop's CEO, described the app's users in a newspaper interview in 2019, "They are in that period of their lives where they are figuring out for themselves what they want to do in the future, and we want to give them an opportunity. To support them in their journey."

Precisely the same words apply to Depop itself and its hypergrowth journey. The central question I faced was whether the management team had the ability to deliver on the strategic goals over the next four years. Not only did we expect the business to be many times its current scale, but we expected the business to grow in complexity as it expanded its operations in the US and opened new markets around the world.

Shortly after the deal was closed, my colleague Lindsay Bedard and I spent three days in London with Depop's management team. Our approach typically begins with one-on-one meetings with the CEO and each member of the leadership team. These meetings usually take place over three to four days, providing an opportunity to immerse ourselves in the business. We usually come away with roughly 200 pages of notes from our conversations. After these meetings, we take ten to fourteen days to synthesize our findings and develop an action plan to be shared with the General Atlantic deal team, the CEO, and the Board of Directors, as appropriate. The overall goal is to help build a leadership team that can multiply the increase in total enterprise value, e.g., by >2.5x in four years.

Ahead of the trip, we worked closely with Melis to draft a scorecard for the company to measure and compare key characteristics, leveraging a framework developed by ghSmart, a specialist in this process. The scorecard served as an anchor for our conversations with the team.

When we first arrived at the Depop offices, we were welcomed into the energetic and open floorplan and were shown to a glass conference room. As we waited to start our meetings, we quietly observed the office setting and immediately spotted Maria zipping around the office, engaging and brainstorming with team members at all levels. Many employees chose not to use their dedicated desks, but instead used other nooks in the office to huddle with colleagues. There was electricity in the air, a buzz and excitement across the floor.

Throughout our time on-site, we had multiple conversations with Maria, during which we unpacked her career track record and experience as the CEO of Depop, as well as key strategic priorities for the business, potential challenges, and expectations for each member of her management team. We also spent time with ten members of her management team to understand their experience and accomplishments, as well as get confidential feedback on other members of the leadership team. After the meetings, Lindsay and I went straight to dinner to begin working through our findings, which continued during our flight back to New York. Over the next ten days, we had conversations with other leaders in marketplace businesses and synthesized our findings from the meetings with the team into a thirty-page strategy deck to share and discuss with Maria and Melis.

When we sat back down with Maria, it was clear she was eager to reconnect and hear our findings. Over the two-hour meeting, we walked her through our observations and the supporting data in great detail. While our work is intended to be constructive, it was important to first recognize that Maria and the entire Depop team had created a product and model that were innovative, and that the business had many strengths that needed to be preserved.

From the moment we set foot in the office, the culture came across as entrepreneurial, innovative, and youthful. Throughout our conversations, it became clear that employees were passionate about the brand and took great pride in their work. Employee surveys suggested strong company-wide engagement, with average participation rates above 80 percent. Additionally, Depop had mastered engaging the Gen Z customer base through creative events and partnerships. It was doing so well that it had invested only limited amounts in paid marketing. The events included a highly successful pop-up store in Selfridges department store in the UK and a live event in the US. This fast, organic growth is rare in consumer tech businesses and often challenging to replicate.

1. Achieve key financial objectives
<ul><li>Deliver [XX%+] revenue growth per annum with high-profitability margins through 2025.</li><li>Revenue: From [$XXmm] in YE 2020 to [$XXXmm] by 2025</li><li>Gross Margin: From [XX%] in YE 2020 to [XX%] by 2025</li><li>Adj. EBITDA Margin: From [XX%] in YE 2020 to [XX%] by 2025</li></ul>
2. Develop and execute strategy for expansion opportunities (geographic and scope of services)
<ul><li>Expand presence in the US. US to contribute [XX%] of total revenue by 2025</li></ul>
3. Build and manage a high-performing team; build a culture of high performance
<ul><li>Build a high-performing team, comprised of <90% A players</li><li>Foster a high-performing culture of ownership and accountability</li></ul>

In addition to developing this strong connection with consumers, the business had developed a good approach for managing its seller community. This included ancillary support services related to shipping, payments, and authentication. Critical in any two-sided marketplace, Depop had developed a sustainable business that effectively balanced supply and demand and a rapidly growing, enthusiastic community of users.

Among the leadership teams, there was unanimous support for Maria as CEO. She was passionate, approachable, warm, and encouraging. Many on her management team told us that she was the primary reason they had joined the company. As is often the case, we focused the first portion of our conversations (about 30 percent of the meetings when we debriefed the relevant stakeholders) on the CEO's strengths and potential areas for development. Even the most seasoned and established CEOs have areas for growth and improvement, and we encourage our CEOs to be relentless in their pursuit of constant and continuous development.

Maria is from Spain and has lived and worked in multiple countries, giving her a strong global orientation and exposure to both established and entrepreneurial environments. She spent five years with Bain & Co. before obtaining her MBA at INSEAD, and later joined Groupon, where she helped expand the business in Japan and South Korea. She joined Depop in 2014 as Vice President of Operations. She was appointed as Depop's CEO in 2016 during a period of turmoil and was credited by her team with restoring order and improving damaged morale.

Maria had, in fact, acted swiftly. Within days of being named CEO, she brought back Depop's founder, Simon Beckerman. Simon was the architect of the Depop brand and shaped its community-driven social experience. Renewing those features was critical to Depop's future, Maria believed. The move was controversial, but Maria was convinced that bringing Simon back would reinvigorate the staff with that founding message. She sensed that Depop's leadership had been operating in silos without a unifying sense of common purpose and that Simon could help recreate the glue to hold them together, while focusing and clarifying the company's sense of identity. She was decisive and put Depop back on its hypergrowth track, energized her leadership teams, and boosted the enthusiasm of her user community, mostly in the UK.

It was a favorable record, but our deal was premised on a rapid scaling up that would increase the challenges on Maria and her teams, especially as they pursued new markets. Our analysis was a critical step in charting that path.

We identified three key impediments to scaling the business. First, while the leadership team was right for the size of the business today, it was underdeveloped relative to where the business needed to go in a short time. Several critical positions had leaders who were light in team management and operating experience. It was an opportune time to redefine and elevate standards of the key executive positions and performance across the company. Second, a recently implemented organizational redesign did not effectively address a significant new ambition, expansion in the US. Third, several key processes and systems were underdeveloped, and priorities changed frequently.

Organization Design Insights

- Optimize for the CEO/Founder's strengths. Ensure that the structure allows for the CEO to focus on the most critical and highest-impact areas.

- As a company scales, there is value in pushing functional aggregation points deeper in the organization. To do this, the company must first build leadership depth, functional excellence, and strong processes and systems. Facebook and Amazon are two such examples where functional aggregation points are found two+ levels below the CEO.

- Functional organization structures are typically efficient and support development of functional excellence; however, they can create barriers for collaboration across boundaries.

- Structure alone will not create success. Governance and cultural elements must be considered and reinforced by the management team. Even the best "hardware" requires the right "software."

We walked Maria through the strengths and suggested development agendas for each member of her team. To her credit, she had successfully tapped a fleet of high-potential leaders, many of whom, like Maria, grew up in consulting and demonstrated strong strategic acumen and impressive intellectual horsepower. That said, few had experience managing a global business of the scale that Depop had already reached, and we felt they would be stretched as Depop grew larger and more complex. Additionally, a few key roles on Maria's team were vacant. More work needed to be done.

At this point, Maria was also actively searching for a Chief Technology Officer and a Chief Product Officer. She was zeroing in on a finalist for CTO, but the pipeline of candidates for the Chief Product Officer was not promising, despite months of work. Additionally, they needed to bring in a high-caliber CFO who had experienced a scaling-up process and who could serve as a strategic partner to Maria. At that moment, Finance was led by a high-potential leader, but she was also straddling Operations. It was not a perfect fit. While exceptionally bright, this individual was stretched thin, and we felt she would benefit from working under a high-quality Finance leader with more experience and a more focused job description.

During our meetings with Maria, we debated the appropriate timeline for hiring a new CFO and ultimately agreed to launch a search immediately. In our experience with growth companies, we have found that the benefits of moving with speed and conviction in filling such key positions far outweigh the potential disruption from what was essentially an upgrade of the job. When we looked at the current state of the Finance function, it was clear that Finance was underserving the organization and that Maria would benefit from promptly bringing in a strategic-minded CFO.

Among the other critical needs was a new performance marketing specialist. Word of mouth had served Depop well in expanding its customer base, but it needed to build heftier performance marketing muscle to support the brand and geographic scaling up. They needed a solid performance marketing leader to partner with the current CMO, who was exceptionally strong in the brand and creative areas. Last, the US General Manager had recently moved back to the UK for personal reasons, which meant there was no dedicated leader on the ground in Depop's most important market.

To prepare for the most productive use of this new talent injection, we worked closely with Maria on both evaluating her organizational design and trying to craft a long-range structure, based on a functional and geographic platform, which would help promote accountability and allow for greater emphasis on the US market. We researched several organization structures and talked with leaders at other companies to help sharpen our thinking and recommendations.

Our collaboration and analysis finally provided what we believed was the right organizational design, and we started working on the implementation plan. We decided

Implementation

	Phase 1: Planning	Phase 2: Workshop	Phase 3: Adoption
Outcome	Align on the optimal organization structure and key staffing decisions	Roles, accountabilities and measures are clearly defined across the enterprise; leaders are clear on their individual and shared accountabilities	Successful adoption, engagement, and performance

Critical Steps	1. **Finalize organization design**
	
	2. **Draft RAMs** (roles, accountabilities and measures) for key positions
	
	3. **Leverage talent to fill new roles & identify critical roles where the necessary capabilities do not exist**
	
	4. **Notify individual leaders of role changes:**
	  i. Communicate mandate and new role
	  ii. Provide leaders with format to present to their peer group during the workshop
		Convene the leadership team for a collaborative dialogue
		
		Agenda to include:
		
		i. Individual presentations on mandate, role, accountabilities, resourcing/capability needs, and cross-functional support areas (extended and expected).
		
		ii. Group discussion on the following:
		  - Individual and shared accountabilities
		  - Nodes
		  - Governance
		  - Operating rhythm
		  - Decision rights and schedule of authorization
		  - Desired leadership markers
			1. **Cascade organizational changes deeper in the organization:**
			  i. Leaders to rescope roles for their respective organizations (RAMs).
			  ii. Leaders to communicate changes to individuals deeper in the organization.
			
			2. **Ensure organizational enablers are installed and maintained:**
			  - Operating rhythm & governance
			  - Performance management
			  - Talent management
			  - Incentives
			
			3. **Measure success and engagement:** Recommend conducting an engagement survey to evaluate the organization's current state and pulse the organization on an annual basis.

Ownership	• CEO to finalize plan and notify leaders. • GA to support CEO in finalizing the design, determining roles & key hires (staging, transition plans & communications) • HR to support drafting RAMs • ELT members to prepare presentations for the workshop	• GA to support CEO in finalizing workshop agenda • CEO to chair and facilitate • HR to help project manage • ELT members to present	• ELT responsible for drafting RAMs for their organization; and communicating changes (HR and CEO to support). • HR to lead performance management, score-carding, and incentive alignment • HR to help project manage

that clear, well-planned communications by Maria to her team was critical to a smooth rollout, in part because of the challenges she had faced in trying to implement a previous reorganization just before the General Atlantic investment. With our support, Maria communicated the proposed changes to individual leaders and then convened the leadership team in a collaborative discussion to create an opportunity for each leader to weigh in, provide feedback, and get more detail on their new roles and how accountability would be handled. Clarity was important so that everyone understood the expectations and the metrics that would be applied to their positions and measure their performance.

Once the new organization structure had been communicated in this step-by-step process, we moved back to the searches for the CFO and Chief Product Officer positions. Fortunately, the CTO finalist we had already been evaluating worked out and Maria extended an offer within weeks. For performance marketing, we decided with Maria to first look for candidates from within the GA Talent Bank, our repository of vetted executives. We had a robust network of promising digital marketing executives to select from.

For the tricky task of recruiting the new CFO and the CPO, we turned to experienced search firms. We knew how much work was required to bring in such new hires in a short time, and we knew that it would be critical to get these hires right. We worked closely with Maria to develop scorecards for the two positions to give us a solid data process for comparing candidates. We also partnered with Russell Reynolds Associates for the CFO search and engaged True Search for the CPO search.

In our initial conversations with Russell Reynolds, we stressed the importance of attracting a high-caliber strategic CFO to assume the critical role of being a strong financial partner to Maria as Depop underwent the stresses of expansion. The first slate of candidates did not meet our standards. What became clear was that the search firm was calibrating the type of candidate to Depop's current size, rather than the significantly greater scale expected in the coming years. We worked quickly to get the search on a better track by discussing our concerns and needs with the search firm. Within days, a more senior Russell Reynolds consultant was brought in to oversee the process.

Over the following months, we assisted Maria by joining the search status calls and providing deep, two-hour assessments with all the candidates for the two positions. This allowed Maria to spend her time not just interviewing top candidates but also building rapport with them and getting the candidates excited about Depop and its business. After four months, we felt confident we had identified the finalist and moved quickly to conduct extensive referencing, prepare a compelling offer, and, finally, close the deal with our lead candidate.

For the CPO position, which would be at the senior vice president level, we relaunched the search with True, which had deep relationships both in the US, a major business focus, and the UK. Within four months, we were able to recruit a product leader from TripAdvisor who, though based in the US, was willing to relocate to Depop's London headquarters. To add additional strength in product development, we also helped Maria identify from the GA Talent Bank and appoint to the Board of Directors a seasoned product executive. This appointment was followed, in early 2021, with an additional female Independent Director, lifting the Board's mix to 50 percent female.

Digital marketing was another critical area that required fresh thinking to support Depop's growth. One of the most positive features of Depop's initial popularity was how word spread organically, largely by word of mouth. Its marketing spend, which was modest, focused on brand awareness rather than customer acquisition. Now that Depop was seeking major expansion in the US, there was a greater need to develop growth marketing capabilities. When assessing marketing leaders, we typically find that they are often oriented toward either brand/creative or performance/growth marketing. While both fall under the umbrella of marketing, they require quite different skill sets, and it is often challenging to find a leader who is adept at both. At times you will find a marketing leader with what is, in effect, a "major" in brand marketing and a "minor" in performance marketing, or vice versa. In Depop's case, Maria had recently recruited a strong brand/creative marketer out of Google. He was the first to admit that growth marketing was not in his wheelhouse and that he would need support in this area.

Structurally, we suggested that Maria consider separating brand and performance marketing, and hire the performance marketing leader as a peer to the CMO. We feared that if this person were more junior and did not have a seat at the leadership table, we would not be able to attract the same caliber of talent. We also determined to target a "digital native" rather than a "digital immigrant," meaning we would look for younger candidates with deep analytical acumen and expertise across a variety of digital channels, even if it meant finding someone with fewer years of professional experience. We discussed this approach with Maria and began identifying and introducing Maria to candidates from our network. Fortunately, we were able to source a highly capable and data-oriented marketing leader.

This talent process was time-consuming but rewarding. Within eight months, Depop significantly strengthened the leadership team and aligned the organization structure to the business strategy, making it well-equipped to flourish during the 2020 pandemic. The pandemic has left wreckage across many business sectors, such as hospitality, airlines, retail, and entertainment. But with people largely confined to their homes, some e-commerce businesses have thrived. Depop has been among them.

Depop's top-line and underlying metrics accelerated meaningfully in 2020, and growth has been sustained in key markets through the lockdowns, even after stimulus payments ended. In 2020, growth merchandise sales were $650 million and revenue reached $70 million, each increasing over 100 percent year over year. The US has grown to 40 percent of total GMV, from 15 percent when Maria started with Depop, and 30 percent when GA made its investment. It is on track to outpace the UK in 2021. On June 2, 2021, just two years after our initial investment, Depop was purchased by Etsy for $1.6 billion, generating a greater than 5"×" multiple in value for General Atlantic and our investors.

KEY LEARNINGS

DEPOP

RAM CHARAN

The case of Depop takes you through a journey of insights into the process that Anish and his team follow when developing a talent strategy, as well as their approach for hiring talent with greater than 90 percent accuracy. The ability to hire talent that can exponentially grow a business is a rare skill that creates enormous value.

- Anish and Lindsay immersed themselves with the management team and led an intensive process to evaluate the company's readiness to deliver on the growth agenda. Their process mimics the same rigor that their investment professionals follow when conducting diligence. Understanding the organization and leadership capacity at a company is the first step to setting up a business for scale.

- This chapter surfaces a common challenge than most high-growth companies face—building a leadership team and organization that is equipped to scale while you're scaling. Fundamental to Anish's approach is hiring talent ahead of the curve. When GA first invested in Depop, revenues were in the teens. During the initial phase of the CFO search, as an example, the search consultant presented candidates who were equipped to handle the company's current scale. Anish supported the CEO with elevating her standards on leadership, and together they focused on finding a CFO who was equipped to handle the scale that the business expected to reach in the next four to five years.

- The Depop story demonstrates the benefit and value of moving quickly, and the impact that strong leadership has on value creation. Aligned with GA's objectives to get the right team in place within the first six months of closing a deal, Anish and Lindsay supported Depop with developing a leadership team that was fit to scale out of the gates. To do this, they immediately plugged themselves into the business, with a process that started even before the deal closed. As soon as General Atlantic invested, Anish and Lindsay flew to London to spend a week on-site with the team, and worked with Maria to develop a talent strategy within the next two weeks. Searches were kicked off immediately after their talent strategy debrief and rigorously managed to ensure they identified the right candidates quickly.

CHAPTER 4

A RISK-TAKING LEADER LIFTS A CORPORATE PHOENIX FROM THE ASHES

VISHAL RETAIL

Perhaps it wasn't the best sign that we first heard about the opportunity to invest in Vishal Retail, a chain of Indian hypermarkets, from one of its banks. The chain of 150 or so stores was in disarray—it was overburdened with debt, unpaid suppliers were in revolt, and sales were collapsing. It was 2009 and Vishal faced the prospect of being liquidated if a new investor didn't step in. Its lenders were desperately looking for a rescue.

I had recently joined the private equity firm TPG, based in the Hong Kong office, and our Asian deal partners decided to have a look. As they examined Vishal, they found a company broken on just about every level. In addition to bleeding cash, the management, made up of the founder, Ram Chandra Agarwal, and family members, was unable to run a company of that size and complexity. Property owners were going unpaid and threatening to evict them. The stores themselves, many of them in smaller towns, had deteriorated, with stale merchandise, broken and dirty fixtures, and poorly trained, underpaid staff. The most memorable feature of my first visit to the head office in New Delhi, when I was invited to do an assessment, was mice skittering by on the floor.

Rodents aside, elements of the mess were interesting, possibly promising. While the company was teetering on the edge of a cliff, it had, just maybe, the potential to be a major breakout investment if some urgent issues could be tackled. Perhaps the most important one was leadership. The challenge started with finding a new CEO, but it also required building an entire leadership team—dozens of senior executives—under exceptionally difficult circumstances if we were to have any kind of a shot at a turnaround while multiplying the value of our investment. But what talented executive would want to join a company confronting so many failures? And even putting a great team in place was no guarantee of success. It would require constant support, coaching, and development of that essential human capital, stretching every capacity of a CHRO.

The deal partners, led by TPG's head of India, Puneet Bhatia, had already been looking at the relatively undeveloped Indian retail sector before hearing about Vishal. They believed the underlying macro factors supported a good opportunity. The basic strategy, put simply, was to get control of a viable chain and bring in world-class management and retailing expertise to implement a scaling-up process and breakout in value. It was a bold vision based on a compelling assessment of India's growing economy.

It began with the fact that, at that time, retailing was almost entirely a local business in India, with thousands of mom-and-pop shops. Despite all the efficiencies that come with scale and rapid growth, chains held a tiny share of the national retailing market. In fact, there were no profitable national hypermarket chains in India at all then. The sector was so young and underdeveloped that the nascent chains that existed were generally unprofitable and lacked the sophistication of retailers in more advanced economies. Bring in international caliber talent and you could start to turn that around, the partners believed.

And India was changing rapidly. The economy was modernizing and, as a result, the lower- and middle-income classes were growing, with more purchasing power. We were convinced that the time was right to develop a chain of hypermarkets, similar to the Walmart or Target models. Vishal, with its 150 or so stores, seemed like it might be an attractive platform to begin that effort and scale it up. Despite its many problems, it had some positive characteristics. It had created strong brand recognition among its mostly lower- and middle-income clientele, and that could be leveraged. Its cost structure was relatively low. Its product mix delivered higher margins than many other hypermarkets. The timing seemed auspicious—if we could stabilize the company's continually declining finances, fend off unpaid lenders, and inject the right leadership.

Private equity investments always rely heavily on finding innovative, disciplined talent, but this opportunity needed steely and creative leadership that understood the Indian consumer and Indian regulations, and was well-versed in modern retailing and marketing. We also needed leaders who could win over both TPG's Investment Committee and the Indian banks that had made loans to Vishal. On top of that, the person had to be capable of overseeing a massive turnaround before scaling up the chain, or it would be a financial disaster, an embarrassment to Puneet and me, and, above all, to TPG.

A key to the investment was Vishal's business model—a focus on lower- and middle-income consumers, who make up a significant majority of India's massive population of 1.35 billion. Some newer Indian retail chains were pursuing a strategy of seeking more affluent customers, but that meant paying much higher rents in more costly neighborhoods and having to carry more expensive inventory for a much smaller customer base. Vishal benefited from lower rents because it put stores where its customers lived. It was a bold strategy, but also highly risky. Puneet was trying to take the ashes of an entrepreneurial effort that was at its nadir and turn it into a type of retail chain that didn't really exist in India.

After a careful evaluation, Puneet and his partners had developed a strong conviction in the prospect of stabilizing Vishal and injecting the right leadership to engineer a rebirth. Once they sketched out their deal thesis and the supporting analysis, they brought the idea to TPG's Investment Committee and shared their enthusiasm.

The committee considered the prospect for just ten minutes and promptly rejected it, leaving no apparent room for reconsideration. We were shocked, but perhaps should not have been.

Not only was Vishal in freefall and tied up in litigation, not only was it a player in a sector that was not developed in India, not only did tough Indian regulations on foreign ownership of retailers complicate any possible transaction, but there also were no obvious places to go within the country to find experienced leaders to run it.

Undeterred, Puneet and another TPG partner, Amol Jain, came to me and asked if I could evaluate the company and its leadership needs, and see if I could build the robust leadership team needed to guide the idea to fruition. I had been at TPG just a few months, but Puneet believed deeply in the significant role talent would play in any turnaround. It was both an opportunity and an enormous challenge, perhaps the riskiest challenge in my career up to that time, and it rested, in part, on the strength of the partnership I would develop with Puneet. We had to climb not one but several mountains together, and we were off to a rough start.

Having worked at TPG for such a brief time, I had not had much of a chance to develop a relationship with Puneet. I sought him out shortly after my arrival so we could begin discussing ways to collaborate, but his jammed schedule made that difficult. When we finally set up a lunch, he brought along several colleagues and departed quickly, leaving little time for me to get acquainted with him. Later, as we began to discuss how I might assist in the Vishal deal, it became clear that this was a high-stakes effort and it would be my responsibility not just to evaluate, identify, and recruit high-quality talent but to win Puneet's trust in my ability to deliver. We shared a common view that, to a large degree, this deal would be talent-driven.

I was eager to get started and was ready—except that there was no budget to begin hunting for the uniquely capable leadership we required. Also, we did not actually own the company, and there was no guarantee we ever would.

I was coming around to the vast opportunity that Vishal represented, but I was realistic as I assessed how I could go about finding the talent we desperately needed. One of the biggest hurdles was that, since India had such a poorly organized retailing sector and so few successful national chains, there was no obvious deep bench of talent to explore to find CEO candidates, or the rest of the leadership team. We needed executives with the necessary background in data-driven merchandising, marketing, compliance, financial, and operational capabilities. We also needed someone with the steely nerves and skill to produce a turnaround—in other words, a real business athlete.

I grew up in India and received my education in business and human resources there, and I had worked initially for PepsiCo, helping in its ambitious efforts to scale up its business in the country. It provided excellent training. I played a role in helping the company sharply expand its market share from roughly 10 percent to 40 percent in three years. More importantly, I had created a talent program in which I brought in experienced executives from other countries both to help manage our business and to train promising Indian staff, turning out capable world-class managers. The PepsiCo experience gave me a deeper understanding of how I could go about identifying and developing talent to support our potential investment in Vishal.

Under normal circumstances, I would tackle these issues within months of the firm's making an investment in a portfolio company. With Vishal, I had to build the team just to get past the TPG Investment Committee before taking ownership. I had to persuade Puneet, the other members of the deal team, and then the Investment Committee that we had the right people available just to have any kind of shot at getting a green light to acquire Vishal.

The first tentative step in my process was persuading a search firm, Heidrick & Struggles, to begin the CEO search, but there was a twist. I explained that we had no money and no company, at least not yet. Of course, we had a long relationship, and they knew we did a substantial amount of executive search business, and I explained why we believed this was a promising idea. They would be working for free, at least initially, with a promise of compensation if and when we succeeded. It was a gamble, but I was eventually able to persuade them to take on the unusual assignment.

Within weeks they came back with some viable local and global candidates. One of them was Gunender Kapur, known as GK, a highly talented executive with experience in the consumer sector. He had previously worked in executive positions at Hindustan Lever, the Indian subsidiary of the giant European consumer goods company Unilever.

The company is highly respected in India for its excellent management and management training program, and GK had worked his way up through several positions and eventually served on its executive committee. What was particularly important to me was that he had led the turnaround of a food division there, an essential skill for the Vishal position, and that he had led the successful scaling up of their oral care products business. He also had strong experience in hiring and building a leadership team. He was the kind of business athlete we needed, with a broad set of skills and a deep understanding of the Indian economy. He was decisive and had a reputation for applying high standards for himself and his team.

After GK left Lever, he became the president and CEO of a unit of Reliance Retail, a division of the big Indian conglomerate Reliance Industries Limited. This gave him significant experience in growing a business, in this case, supermarkets; at one point he was opening a store a day for the business in India. That, too, was essential to our plan for Vishal. Overall, he was light in direct retailing experience, but his other capabilities and experience impressed me. He was a disciplined manager and had turned around troubled businesses. We would be betting on his considerable background and potential rather than his résumé as a serial retailer.

Also, his personal character was strong. When we first met—a one-and-a-half-hour conversation—I was particularly impressed that he seemed down to earth and confident; unlike some of the other candidates I was seeing, he made no effort to come across as exceedingly polished, nor did he put on airs. He seemed comfortable in his skin and ambitious, a natural leader. While conveying a sense of humility, he was also clearly a man of integrity and displayed a strong moral compass. I was careful to meet with GK in different settings so I could see how he responded to his environment and to see if he relaxed in less-formal settings. These included everything from formal interview sessions to breakfast meetings and meetings at hotels.

Often, companies regard referencing as routine and devote just a few minutes to asking basic questions. I take a different approach and often spend forty-five minutes or more on each reference call so that I can probe and seek information on how the executives have performed in difficult situations and how they have built and led their teams, and to get a sense of their character. GK's references were quite strong and strengthened my sense that he was the leader we needed.

I provided detailed notes on all my encounters to Puneet, which required synthesizing my fifty pages of written notes into a two-page summary. I wanted to make sure he understood the depth of my analysis and how I evaluated critical factors, and that he understood the scorecards I created, showing how the candidates compared. I seized the opportunity to make certain he understood my methods.

I pursued this process with more than a dozen candidates but, increasingly, GK stood out, even with the level of industry experience. We discussed the Vishal Retail opportunity and GK expressed interest. I made it clear that this investment carried big risks for him personally. Under our strategy, he would become a Senior Adviser to TPG, analyzing the company for himself, assembling a leadership team to run Vishal, and formulating a business plan that, unless everything went right, he might never be able to implement. His pay initially would be a fraction of what he was earning at Reliance, though there was the possibility of his earning significantly more, many millions of dollars more, if TPG did the deal and GK delivered the multiples in value we were banking on.

GK had an important hidden desire. He said that he had had a dream for years of wanting to build and lead a major corporation on his own. He had an entrepreneurial spirit and wanted a sense of ownership. Without access to the kind of capital required to create such an opportunity from the ground up, the Vishal deal would be, he said, something of a once-in-a-lifetime opportunity to reach that aspiration at such a scale, since a major part of his incentive pay would include an ownership stake, alongside TPG's.

I was becoming convinced that he was our best candidate, but I had to satisfy many people, so the process was demanding. We put him through more than fifteen interviews, including with members of the TPG Investment Committee. The meetings with Puneet were a particularly difficult test, both of GK and our relationship. But I was convinced that his exceptional skills, decisive leadership style, and high standards were what Vishal needed.

Puneet recognized that GK had many strengths, but continued to wonder if we needed someone with more direct experience in retail and with hypermarkets. He understood that, in private equity, if you get the leadership and human capital wrong, little else can rescue an investment. Talent can be the difference between multiplying value or getting egg on your face. I had to defend my analysis while acknowledging that we would have to work on these questions. I made sure that I gave Puneet substantial information on how GK compared with the other leading candidates, how he had performed in interviews, the relevance of his background—

particularly with turning around a business and scaling up another—and the importance his strong character would have in helping the company navigate its poor morale, angry staff, and anxious banks. Over time, Puneet came to trust me and the thoroughness of the process I had put in place.

At the same time, GK was also looking at opportunities with several PE firms. The interaction with all the TPG colleagues in this process gave him the confidence that TPG would be the best partners for him. After two months, we agreed to hire GK and began the even harder work of pre-assembling an entire management structure, which would require hiring more than thirty people over the years to come.

After we finalized our decision on GK, we needed to obtain approval from TPG's Investment Committee. That would require more than twenty presentations over the span of a year, some of them by GK as he sought to persuade the committee that he had a strong vision and the ability to carry it out. Certainly, the opportunity looked crystal clear—but that was on paper. For me, it meant providing detailed updates on my several dozen searches, and my analyses. On numerous occasions, I took the red-eye flight from Hong Kong to New Delhi and had to go directly to the presentations to ensure that the committee understood both exactly where we were and my methodology.

As we neared the end of our first year, examining all aspects of Vishal, discussing possible deals with its banks, and developing the operating plan, we found that the

TPG Investment Committee, though so resistant at first, appreciated our updates and our progress.

But as the months stretched out, our biggest problem was that Vishal was unraveling fast. Revenues had fallen by half over the previous sixteen months, to about $60 million. The banks, which had been forced to step in and exert control in the effort to salvage their loans, vehemently disagreed on what sort of plan they might accept, adding to the uncertainty. The TPG Investment Committee finally said they feared there were too many obstacles. They expressed appreciation for what they described as a great journey, but indicated it might be time to cut our losses and move on, not wasting any more time. Trying to deal with Vishal was like catching a falling knife: tremendous risks were obscuring the potential rewards. Puneet and the rest of the deal team acknowledged the problems, but their conviction was as strong as ever. They kept coming back to the extremely strong macro factors that still made the investment attractive.

Vishal's story retained the same powerful elements: the chain focused on lower-income families, a huge consumer group; stores were located in less-affluent towns and neighborhoods, where rents and other costs were significantly lower than big cities; the brand was popular; it was the second-largest hypermarket chain in India; and its product mix, weighted toward higher-margin merchandise such as apparel, rather than food, held the prospect of high returns and growth. Being so distressed also meant we could acquire it at a big discount. Having GK on board strengthened our arguments.

Puneet insisted that the pioneering deal could make history in India. Another TPG partner, Carlos Aquino, a highly regarded expert in operations, was growing frustrated with the Investment Committee's hesitation and argued that, because of the immensely favorable macro factors, success would be "like falling out of bed."

Finally, as Vishal's banks grew more anxious, we negotiated a deal that both sides could live with. The Investment Committee came around to the view that, with Vishal deteriorating, it was now or never. They chose now because of our conviction and the amount of work we had already done in assembling a high-quality leadership team under GK. With that initial financial restructuring agreed on, and GK having proved his capabilities, the committee approved the complex investment in Vishal at the beginning of 2011.

Even so, many pieces still had to come together to get this to the finish line. The deal structure had to dance around Indian retail business regulations. Foreign companies were not permitted to own the stores, so we constructed a two-part structure in which a partner, India's Shriram Group, acquired the retail end of the business—the stores—and TPG acquired the wholesale part of the business, including the central administration, so that we controlled the overall strategy, including finances, merchandising, and marketing. Through our negotiations with the many banks, we arranged to repay them about 40 cents on the dollar for their loans and provided enough working capital to get Vishal restarted.

The critical piece was supporting GK in selecting and installing the leadership team. It had been a painstaking process to ensure that the team could bring world-class capabilities to the venture. For each open role, we looked within GK's network, my own talent network, TPG's network, or working with referrals and search firms to identify leaders capable of excelling in this environment. By the time we closed the transaction, GK, with our support, had lined up nearly 70 percent of the leadership team. They included:

- The head of apparel, a particularly talented retailer and a critical position since those sales made up about 55 percent of revenues;

- The head of a fast-moving consumer goods business, an accomplished leader sourced from GK's network;

- The head of HR, sourced through my Talent Bank;

- The Controller, a highly experienced person to take over financial reporting and accounting, who was sourced from GK's network; and

- The head of marketing, whom we identified and signed up in advance and who resigned from her prior position to join Vishal the day the deal closed.

Unlike some other hypermarkets, which rely on food and other fast-moving consumer goods for a substantial portion of their sales, Vishal's largest sales category is apparel. It is one of the strategic factors that contributed to our optimism. Fast-moving consumer goods have low margins and thus are a poor match for the high rents these stores often must bear. At Vishal, around 25 percent of revenues are from fast-moving consumer goods and food. Apparel is a much higher margin, and thus it amplifies the benefits of the lower rents Vishal stores pay because of its locations in lower-income towns and neighborhoods.

That is why finding a strong candidate to lead the apparel business and refurbish Vishal's product lines had been vital. Vishal interviewed nearly twenty people, and GK was fortunate to find an experienced, highly capable woman for the position. She lived in Mumbai, and Vishal had to sweeten the package to make it attractive for her to move to New Delhi.

Once the deal had been completed and GK moved into action, he continued to recruit talent to fill out the team. One of the most critical was the new CFO. This was a challenge. The first candidate lost support over time, and the next favorite ended up showing interest but backing out because of the risks. We then identified a strong candidate, working in Singapore at that time as the CFO at Unza, a consumer business that was a subsidiary of Wipro. GK knew him and had introduced him to us. I flew to Singapore both to evaluate him and to sell him on our plan. Over the course of three weeks, GK and I had multiple meetings with him, and we also had others from TPG spend time with him as well to ensure we all had full conviction that he was the right person.

GK took a novel approach to putting strong operations leaders in place. First, he found an executive in India who had the right qualifications and had worked with GK, and we gave him responsibility for half the country. Then we found an executive from Sam's Club with strong operations experience, again someone who had worked with GK, and placed him in charge of the other half of the country. But, to ensure coordination, GK placed them in the same office in Delhi. GK would later hire, above them, a COO from Walmart.

In our efforts to introduce strong senior-level management capabilities from more developed markets, we also recruited Board-level advisers drawn from our talent networks. They played an important role in supporting GK to complement his strengths. We brought in Jonathan Price, who had previously worked at The Body Shop and Best Buy, to assist in the retailing operations. We also engaged Steve Johnson from my network, who came from the Asda supermarket chain in the UK and the Russian hypermarket chain Lenta. We also brought in Matthew Rubel, the former Chairman of Collective Brands, who was an adviser at TPG.

This was a promising start, and we believed we were finding the talent we needed to transform the business and give GK everything he needed to succeed and implement his vision. His approach hinged on several observations about India's changing consumers and the growing middle class. Not only was a rapidly modernizing economy building a middle class with more disposable income, but the internet revolution was having a big impact on the tastes and dreams of those people, many just emerging from poverty. They were developing new aspirations for the kind of life they wanted to live, how they wanted to dress and look, influenced by widely accessible images of Western styles on the internet.

GK's strategy was to give lower-income consumers access to those fashions at prices they could afford. In addition, he worked closely with suppliers to ensure that quality was high. Bolstering this approach was the liberal, no-questions-asked return policy he instituted. He appreciated that, for a poor Indian consumer, the purchase of an article of clothing that fell apart quickly or was ill-fitting could be a real financial setback, so he developed Vishal's policies to win loyalty.

GK's plan lifted our own aspirations for Vishal Retail, but, however lofty the vision, we had to contend with a much darker, chaotic environment once our boots hit the ground. Even the best talent cannot inoculate a business from having to navigate unexpected disasters and challenges, and Vishal's first year presented an unending string of such problems.

In GK's initial efforts to get control of the chain, he acted immediately to slow the cash drain. He closed thirty of the 150 stores in just weeks. We had conducted a deep analysis and determined that the stores were not situated properly to support the strategy. GK planned on scaling up later, but to start we had to prevent losses on stores that showed little if any prospect of turning profits. GK also replaced about a third of the employees within the first six months and nearly 90 percent within the first two years.

Day-to-day issues and the poor organization we inherited consumed us. GK instituted a temporary system that required that he personally approve every expenditure for the first ninety days. It was cumbersome but, he believed, essential to putting some order into the system and preventing inappropriate transactions. Then there was the litigation we inherited. GK needed to deal with lawyers and summons constantly and in numerous locations, given India's fragmented legal system. Most came from suppliers and vendors, unpaid for months if not years, and some had grown tired waiting for the courts to act. More than once, some showed up in the Vishal offices with armed guards, demanding payment. The situation grew so threatening that we created a hidden back door in the main offices so GK and his leadership could slip out if threatening visitors showed up.

At one point, an unpaid vendor managed to obtain a nonbailable arrest warrant for GK, Amol Jain, and Puneet. Our lawyer contacted us and urged that, if we were out of India, we not enter for the time being, and, if in the country, to lie low and not appear publicly. These were not the usual procedures in the private equity playbook. We believed that this was just a scare tactic and that the warrant had been obtained inappropriately. Our lawyers had the warrant lifted, but the incident spoke volumes about the potential for chaos at Vishal.

Compliance with local regulations also presented painstaking attention. Retail stores are required to comply with as many as thirty local laws and regulations, and some permits must be renewed monthly. Under the previous management, the process had been neglected. GK established a chart listing the approvals and licenses needed, with those unfulfilled marked in red. Initially, nearly the entire chart was red, but, through a methodical process, he eliminated the problems one by one and brought the stores into compliance.

While working to improvise solutions to those problems—which also included lengthy negotiations with owners of stores who had gone unpaid—GK took a number of strategic steps. A key effort was finding ways to dispose of stale merchandise so that it could be replaced with more up-to-date, higher-quality products, particularly apparel. All the old merchandise generally had to be unloaded at steep discounts just to clear the way, a time-consuming process.

The first year was an almost daily battle for survival. Nearly every brick of the business had to be rebuilt, even reimagined. But by the end of that year the company was breaking even, same-store sales were generally rising, many lenders were starting to get repaid, and, by clearing out old merchandise, Vishal was bringing in merchandise that was better quality and more fashionable, which attracted more shoppers.

GK had cleaned and upgraded the look of the remaining stores and had taken another significant step to make the shopping experience more customer-friendly: removing the bottlenecks at the checkout lines. Vishal introduced handheld mobile payment devices, an innovative step at that time in India. Associates with the devices spread out, creating significantly more capacity to speed checkout payments and get customers on their way.

Having achieved those milestones, GK began opening new stores at well-researched locations in Year Two, starting the essential scaling-up process. Every new store meant creating roughly a hundred jobs, so entering the expansion phase helped us boost revenues, drive productivity, and earn employee loyalty. But the strains of growth also tested the leadership and required replacing some senior executives who were not working out.

A Board member we had brought in seemed bureaucratic and inflexible, so we made the decision to replace him. Another critical talent issue arose when the Indian woman GK had hired to head the apparel division decided to leave the company to return to her family's home in Mumbai after several productive years. She had had real impact on the business, and we were eager to bring in world-class talent to maintain momentum. Eventually, Vishal found an experienced retailer in London, and then another talented apparel executive from Paris who was working in China, who added new sophistication and productivity to Vishal's business. She was data-driven and continued to upgrade the merchandise in this high-margin area.

The Vishal Board, which I had joined as the head of the Remuneration Committee, met quarterly, but we had set up a system of monthly meetings with a Board executive committee to make sure we were monitoring the business closely and responding to problems rapidly. I spent time with GK to discuss his progress and offer support as needed before and after those meetings to make sure I understood his challenges and to offer resources that might be useful. I coordinated with Puneet, keeping him closely informed, getting his feedback, and then sharing our feedback with GK to make sure he understood the Board's priorities. I also led two performance reviews a year with GK, focusing on business indicators, his needs and achievements, and also his objectives for the coming year. Once a year, these conversations included his annual compensation and incentive program. This was critical to our communication and ensured that our process was analytical.

TPG followed up its initial investment with two additional tranches to provide capital for growth, and the pace of expansion accelerated, creating strong increases in value. Productivity and revenues increased sharply as Vishal added new stores and increased same-store sales. EBITDA more than doubled from Years Four to Six after we had made our initial investment.

By 2018, Vishal Retail was a different company. It had become the fastest-growing retailer in India and the country's largest retailer of apparel. Imitators had sprung up, a reflection of the strength of Vishal's hypermarket model, but our combination of rapid growth and relatively low costs strengthened the brand and produced continued increases in the multiplying value of the enterprise.

TPG decided to exit this once high-risk investment at the end of 2018, selling its shares to some of the investment partners who had come on board. A company that had about $60 million in annual revenue in 2011 had grown to over $800 million in revenues, was highly profitable, and had expanded to 370 stores across the country. Perhaps just as satisfying, it employed more than 13,000 people directly, and 100,000 indirectly, at vendors and suppliers, many of them semi-skilled workers now receiving significantly higher wages than in the past. In building Vishal's leadership team, I had personally conducted nearly 200 interviews. It was extremely rewarding to see that my methodology had helped create the foundation for this remarkable success. GK's leadership and vision had delivered impressive performance, and he remains an investor and CEO as Vishal continues its upward trajectory, not just a valuable investment but a sustained business and social success.

KEY LEARNINGS

VISHAL RETAIL

RAM CHARAN

This was a company everyone was ready to dump in the trash. The banks had given up hope. However, Puneet and the rest of the deal team were convinced that there was significant opportunity to create substantial value from the business. As a partner to the deal team, Anish was not going to let a lack of talent be the reason to walk away from the deal.

- In looking for a CEO, Anish and the deal team understood that they could not get everything on their checklist. Individuals with substantial retail experience in India did not exist. What they found with GK, however, was someone with a very strong performance track record, deep understanding of the Indian consumer, and incredible potential and leadership skills. In a sector that was underdeveloped, there was never going to be a candidate who checked every box, so they surrounded GK with the right advisers, Board members, and key leaders to ramp up quickly.

- GK, with Anish's support, knew he needed to build a team with a skillset that complemented his, so his focus was on bringing in leaders from the retail sector. While they may not have had experience in India, GK brought that in spades. In turn, they brought the global retail experience that GK was light on at the time. It is vital to surround high-potential talent in critical roles with other leaders who bring complementary skills.

- Notably, GK took a lot of risk. He was in a comfortable, senior role at Reliance Retail, but he had a desire to lead a major company on his own. He took a leap of faith by taking an advisory position with TPG, which could ultimately give him the chance of being the CEO at Vishal and building India's first hypermarket. This is a lesson for all leaders. It is easy to get caught up in the trappings of day-to-day corporate life, but the great leaders are in touch with their own desires and mission and use that to fuel them onto better things.

- Anish was innovative, starting the talent search process even before investing in Vishal. He persuaded a search firm to begin work without compensation, relied on his own talent network in Asia, and earned the trust of his investing colleagues. He engaged in hundreds of detailed interviews with pages and pages of notes and ultimately arranged for a highly capable executive to agree to come in as CEO for a company before the investment could be approved and finalized. He partnered with the deal team and GK in building out a strong team. Ultimately, his perseverance paid off with an incredibly successful outcome for TPG and Vishal.

CHAPTER 5

PUTTING TALENT AND COLLABORATION FIRST TO DRIVE VALUE CREATION

ALEX GORSKY, CHAIRMAN & CEO, JOHNSON & JOHNSON

When he took over as the CEO of venerable Johnson & Johnson in April 2012, Alex Gorsky brought much more than years of experience in the pharmaceutical industry and an impressive track record. He brought a jolt of fresh energy in the form of strong new commitments to innovation and collaboration that allowed this West Point graduate and Army veteran to transform the company so that it acts, as he has put it, like a "135-year-old start-up."

He has broken down old silos, created a sense of entrepreneurialism and ownership among managers, opened the culture by embracing promising research ideas from outside the company as well as inside, and inspired his leadership to think broadly about the entire enterprise rather than any single division. He has demonstrated that even an extremely large, older company can create value like a nimble newcomer with an injection of entrepreneurial spirit. It is an elephant that dances, and the results speak for themselves.

Since Alex took over as head of the company, Johnson & Johnson's market cap has grown by almost $300 billion and has generated returns of about 150 percent, triple the performance of an index of the big pharmaceutical companies.[1] He has, in short, created multiples in value, much like a high-growth equity-backed business.

As he explained in a conversation, one key to Alex's many years of success is how he reconceptualized and oversaw the role of talent at the company and fostered a sense of accountability and collaboration. That took, he says, a new kind of leader. He rewrote the company's Talent Playbook to make it more suited to a changing world and rapidly shifting, highly competitive markets.

What has he done differently?

He pulled his leadership team out of its traditional silos and encouraged the executives to think in a more integrated

---

1   Per S&P's Capital IQ. Based on a custom index comprised of Novartis, Roche, GlaxoSmithKline, Merck, Pfizer, and Bristol Myers Squibb measured from April 26, 2012, to February 26, 2021.

way about the intersection of critical functions rather than in isolation from each other. As a result, Johnson & Johnson scientists think more about the commercialization of products, and commercial leaders are urged to learn more about the science behind drugs and devices and how they are developed. This mindset is pushed deeper into the organization, with executives thinking horizontally about the company's overall success, not just their own divisions.

This reinvention has changed the traditional paradigm of scientific leaders at the company. Alex said he has urged them to "think of themselves as occupying a dual role that is equal parts research and strategic leadership." This has contributed to the erosion of the traditional boundaries between the business side of the company and the R&D side.

One concrete step he initiated was to join the research and development leaders and commercialization leaders as co-heads of key divisions, because of the acceleration in the speed of changes in markets and the needs for new drugs and health products. This "two in a box" approach is not new, but what made a difference is getting the two operating in a harmonized rhythm. This model has unlocked a stronger sense of accountability and collaboration across the enterprise.

"We've seen more innovation in the past five years than in the previous thirty combined," he said. "To keep up with this incredible pace of transformation, we developed a high-performing co-leadership structure that aligns the R&D and commercial functions."

This model was implemented at the top, and also cascaded deeper into specific divisions, such as therapeutics. "If you look at our therapeutic areas such as immunology, we have an R&D head and commercial head who work in tandem and have achieved great results," he said. "Across our entire family of companies, this model has unlocked a new spirit of entrepreneurship, innovation, and accountability that is driving enterprise-wide growth."

In the "two in a box" model, the R&D and Commercial leaders share joint accountabilities and must appreciate and rely on one another to drive the success and growth of the unit. "To make this work, we had to create the right environment, set the right expectations and incentives, and implement the right development systems."

Alex has focused on recruiting and developing talent that is capable of looking beyond boundaries. He has transformed the traditional pharmaceutical approach of seeking only innovative new products from in-house research, and instead has encouraged the organization to be just as aggressive in pursuing new ideas acquired from outside sources.

"We are deeply committed to our internal R&D, but at the same time we prioritize creating the most robust innovation ecosystem we can, be it through organic growth and innovation, partnership, or acquisition. We call it being 'innovation agnostic,' and that allows you to focus on the best possible science and innovation regardless of source. The science is developing so quickly, that, in order to thrive, you need to be agile, capable of identifying interesting, promising, differentiated new platforms. At Johnson & Johnson, we couple that with our size and scale to rapidly bring solutions to a global market."

This new philosophy has required developing and promoting leaders with a different mindset from the past, Alex explained. They must be nimbler, have a deeper understanding of multiple subject areas, and be comfortable working across disciplines. They must love working with great new ideas without concern for where the ideas originated, and they can no longer just be subject matter experts in a single field.

"Today's environment is more dynamic, demanding, and diverse than ever before," he said. "To seize this incredible moment in healthcare, our leaders need to be as good at partnering externally as they are internally. What we are looking to create are situations where all sides realize significant return and significant roles, so everyone is truly invested in success."

Using these acquisitions, many around $100 million, to create billion-plus dollar platforms, has been instrumental in creating significant enterprise value. "This is part of the secret sauce of Johnson & Johnson," Alex said.

Another element in Alex's approach is an intense focus on execution. Leaders at Johnson & Johnson cannot just delegate the execution of plans to lower-level executives, as they might have in the past, but must immerse themselves in all details of implementation.

"Gone are the days when leaders only set the strategy and rely on their teams to execute," Alex said. "The environment is changing so fast, you need constant situational awareness," he said. "Otherwise, a strategic shift will leapfrog you, or an executional failure will suddenly put your entire strategy at risk. For any leader, placing a dual emphasis on strategy and execution is vitally important to success."

Importantly, he has developed an operating rhythm that encourages his leaders to seek and provide feedback to their peers, even on issues that might fall outside their specific areas of responsibility or expertise. Alex himself challenges those leaders and gives them timely and direct feedback. Managers incentivize their teams to think horizontally across the company to build better coordination and collaborative thinking.

All these changes in the kind of talent Johnson & Johnson relies on ultimately requires a new breed of CHRO. The new CHRO must be far more engaged with company leaders and be a partner in overall business performance, not just focused on administrative tasks, Alex said. A successful CHRO now requires "the right balance of empathy and sense of urgency" to change the organization as needed and must be approachable. The CHRO must be a trusted adviser to the CEO and leadership team. Alex said he has built precisely that kind of relationship with his CHRO, Peter Fasolo.

"It's a rare day that Peter is not the first and last person I talk to," Alex said. "We have a relationship that's completely predicated on trust and respect for each other.

I feel completely confident and comfortable having any conversation with him because I know, in the end, both of us are trying to anticipate what's best for the organization."

Alex said he encourages his leadership team to build a close relationship with Peter and confide in him as an adviser on major decisions. "The CHRO needs to be someone that people trust instinctively," he said. "I tell Peter if our business leaders aren't calling him every day, we're in trouble. People turn to Peter because he adds value."

Alex's vision has improved the pace of decision-making at Johnson & Johnson. This also applies to his own decisions related to talent. "Once you realize you've hired or backed the right leader, focus on helping them be successful and able to rise to the occasion. In fact, when I evaluate new leaders, one of the first questions I always ask is how many successful leaders and teams have you supported, how many people owe their careers to you?"

When the pandemic hit in late 2019, Johnson & Johnson immediately started developing a vaccine for the coronavirus, a "moonshot," Alex said. The company assembled what was, in essence, a new operation to drive its research efforts with exceptional speed and its scientists leaped at the opportunity. A close and dynamic partnership between Alex and Dr. Paul Stoffels, Vice Chairman of the Executive Committee and Chief Scientific Officer at Johnson & Johnson, rested at the heart of Johnson & Johnson's response.

"Dr. Stoffels's transformative leadership and ability to get the very best out of his team was a huge reason we were able to undertake such an extraordinary operation," Alex said. "It was a case where our scientists really stepped up under his leadership. They felt a deep commitment to this global health emergency, as we all did at Johnson & Johnson. In January 2020, Dr. Stoffels played an instrumental role in helping our scientists go from receipt of the genomic sequencing information to, literally within a matter of weeks, come up with three or four different candidates for development."

Alex believes many of the lessons here have enduring relevance, far beyond just addressing the COVID-19 pandemic. The partnership between Johnson & Johnson's leaders is a model for how businesses can blend science, innovation, and purposeful leadership to address some of society's most complex problems. "It was a reaffirming moment for how we can use our scale, reach, and expertise to make decisions and products that have enduring positive impact for billions around the globe and generate long-term value for all our stakeholders," Alex said.

To provide the best talent for overseeing this effort alongside Dr. Stoffels, Johnson & Johnson contacted a retired executive and persuaded him to return because of his special expertise in this kind of operational effort. The executive, Jack Peters, who had been Group Chairman for Europe, already possessed the contacts and skills needed to support distribution and access plans.

"We realized that not only did we have to develop a vaccine, but also a distribution system, a way for the entire world, including developing countries, to access our vaccine.

We partnered with the whole spectrum of international organizations, from the Bill and Melinda Gates Foundation to GAVI," he said. "Going from R&D to developing billions of doses for worldwide distribution in a short period of time is an immense effort. There's no way you could train someone to do this fast enough. You needed somebody who already had all those numbers on their iPhone, and had the trust and confidence of all the people in that network. That was Jack."

This focused effort resulted in the successful approval and launch of a new coronavirus vaccine at the end of February 2021. The vaccine development and rollout is an example of Johnson & Johnson's agility, as well as its strong values-based and purpose-driven culture. As CEO, Alex has built a leadership team and organization that is deeply committed to serving its patients and consumers, and created a system wherein leaders are aligned to the company's credo. This purpose-driven focus combined with a mindset of accountability at every level within the organization, has yielded incredible enterprise success and turned Johnson & Johnson into a "135-year-old start-up."

KEY LEARNINGS

JOHNSON & JOHNSON

RAM CHARAN

Instincts suggest that growth companies are limited to private equity-backed or small-cap companies. In reality, even a large, 135-year-old company can operate with a growth mindset. This is something that Alex Gorsky has instilled at Johnson & Johnson, allowing the company to be as nimble as any start-up. Alex has successfully proven that it's possible to make the elephant dance.

- The bane of large, legacy companies in achieving speed and agility is the silo mentality of leaders reporting to the CEO. Alex successfully joined the two most critical engines of growth in one accountability, one business plan, one resource allocation model, one compensation plan, and one set of decisions for the "right people in the right jobs." Nothing is left in the open space between the two that can chew up the CEO's time. Similarly, companies themselves can no longer operate in silos. Alex encourages his leadership team to be open to new ideas, even if they come externally, leading to partnerships and acquisitions with other companies, breaking free from the norms of developing everything in-house. This notion of working across boundaries is a significant market cap multiplier for Johnson & Johnson.

- Alex's partnership with Peter, his CHRO, exemplifies the strategic impact that a high-quality CHRO can make. It was striking to hear that Peter is typically the first and last person he speaks with every day. Peter unlocks value for, and is sought out by, his peers and other functional leaders. He does not just use his role to push policies and procedures throughout the organization. He is a sparring partner to Alex and brings sound judgment on critical talent decisions, organizational design, and incentives. CHROs should think of their role in relation to the pull they generate from other leaders in the business and the value they can create by partnering with them.

- Alex holds all his leaders to extraordinarily high standards. To be successful at Johnson & Johnson, you have to be exceptional at strategy but at the same time, immerse yourself in detail and nail execution. Executives on the leadership team are all aligned in terms of direction and incentives and in challenging each other. All CEOs should hold their teams to these standards and ask them to be as strong in execution as they are in strategy and setting direction.

CHAPTER 6

RETHINKING THE MYTH "IF IT AIN'T BROKE, DON'T FIX IT"

HEMNET

It was a Monday morning, the middle of winter in Stockholm, and my colleague and I were stuck outside the front door of the building where we were holding our first meetings with one of the newest companies in General Atlantic's investment portfolio, Hemnet AB. We were freezing. After buzzing, waiting, and buzzing a few more times, we were finally let in and offered friendly greetings as we began to thaw. But we were given no time to relax and rest before my interviews with the company's leadership team. Within minutes, the company's CEO invited me to address a town hall-type meeting with the employees. With no time to prepare, I improvised and conveyed my excitement about GA's investment in Hemnet and in partnering with the management team to scale up the company. Once settled after that introduction, I then started my first one-on-one evaluation with the CEO, a three-hour conversation.

It was early 2017 and General Atlantic had recently invested in Hemnet, Sweden's dominant online site for real estate listings. It had not been easy. A Norwegian company had got a lock on making the investment earlier in 2016, but regulators had halted that deal out of antitrust concerns. Once the process was reopened, the General Atlantic partner who was the architect of the transaction, Chris Caulkin, moved quickly. Chris is highly experienced in the online classifieds space. He had led investments in SeLoger in France and Immoweb in Belgium, among others. Over the years, Chris has looked at hundreds of online classifieds companies, giving him a strong feel for the industry and an eye for important performance patterns. That allowed him to confidently see that Hemnet was a unique company.

Hemnet holds a dominant position in Sweden's residential home listings business, with a greater than 90 percent market share and about 88 percent awareness among consumers. The entire residential real estate ecosystem relies on this platform. With his strong background, Chris led the negotiations and, finally, the closing of the deal with Hemnet, in which the firm acquired a 61 percent stake, giving this privately held internet company an implicit value of about $214 million.

Hemnet was established in 1998 by two of Sweden's real estate broker associations and the two largest real estate brokerage firms, bringing together residential property buyers and sellers using online tools. Initially, it did not charge for listings, but sold advertising on its website to cover expenses. In 2013, it altered its operating model by charging fees to property sellers for the listings. Hemnet offers a large inventory of properties and access to services for both buyers and sellers, as well as tools to assist brokers in promoting their businesses. The site has about three million visitors a week.

Even with its strong record, we believed Hemnet had untapped potential. We felt it could expand beyond its popular format, developing new lines of related business, making its website more mobile-friendly, and increasing its margins significantly by monetizing its large customer base. It would take an aggressive new plan and a new corporate culture oriented toward product innovation, customer focus, and results. To get there, the company needed a growth-oriented CEO, someone with a desire for change and an entrepreneurial spirit in their DNA.

My meeting that Monday morning with the CEO, whom for the sake of this book I will call John, began on an upbeat note. John was enthusiastic, warm, and engaging. He seemed delighted with General Atlantic's investment.

John had a good track record—Hemnet was performing extremely well—and a story to tell. He was previously a General Manager at a high-growth consumer company and had strong international experience. He had overseen revenue and EBITDA growth at Hemnet and had improved the company's relationship with brokers, who are critical to its success. Earlier, many brokers and sellers had been upset when Hemnet raised its listing fees. But John said he had devoted considerable time meeting and talking with brokers and customers—at least a thousand, he said—to calm their concerns and rebuild trust. This was all quite positive.

When I probed on priorities, John said that his primary priority was to fill vacant positions on his team. Six officers reported directly to him, three heads of business lines and three other senior executives. But, he said, three of the positions had been vacant for some time and, while replacing them was an important objective, it was proving difficult to identify and hire the right candidates. One problem was the size of each unit. At most, they generated slightly more than $20 million a year in revenues, a base that limited the size of the salaries Hemnet could pay, and so limited the candidates they could attract. When John shared this, I pondered a question: why had he continued to recruit for positions that were going to be impossible to fill, rather than rethink the structure to improve his prospects for getting the right talent in place?

When I asked about additional priorities, he said there were few because the prior shareholders had not pressed him to develop other strategic objectives. He was waiting, he said, for the new shareholders to come in, share the growth plan, and help define the new priorities. He explained that he planned to establish a strong set of performance standards for divisions and his executives to ensure there was management accountability, and to cascade the KPIs deeper into the company. These would be built into a performance dashboard that would give a quick snapshot of Hemnet's progress on important goals. Intentions aside, there was no plan ready for launching. He explained that the Board had yet to ask him to do it.

I paused. How was Hemnet proving so successful with half the leadership positions vacant, a lack of clarity on growth priorities, and no system to consistently measure executive performance? I recalled that Chris had said that the culture was not as high performing as he would have liked it to be.

When I sat down with the rest of the management team, I was direct in my questions, which helped me understand the situation. The executives told me that John was a strong believer in achieving consensus, usually a strength. But they feared that this might be inhibiting difficult decisions.

John's strength was interpersonal relationships, both with customers and, to a degree, with Hemnet employees. One consequence was that he tended to avoid taking decisive action or getting involved in issues that might create tensions. He sought collegial relationships with his team: consensus, not conflict. Also, he was quite familiar with consumer tech businesses, but did not have the experience we needed in new product development or in running a strategic planning process. It was becoming clear that there is a difference between a CEO, even a very capable CEO, and a growth CEO. And Hemnet's challenge was growth and change.

After the final interview on our third day, my colleague Camilla Biancardi and I took the 200 pages of annotated notes we had collected and headed to a coffee shop to review what we had learned. It all led us to a question we could no longer avoid: was John the right CEO for the next phase of Hemnet's journey?

With everything we had learned during our three days on-site, our concern was that John did not appear to be the right leader to undertake the demanding job of scaling up the business, disrupting the culture, introducing new product lines, upgrading the technology, and forging a decisive new strategic path in the next leg of Hemnet's corporate journey. The real challenge was to refine our analysis so that we could clearly explain why we had concluded that a CEO delivering solid performance was not the right leader for the future, which, on its face, might have seemed counterintuitive. But it was a message we felt we needed to present to Chris and two other Board members whom we were meeting over dinner later that evening. We had our own difficult decision to make.

We gathered our thoughts and headed into dinner, knowing it would be a potentially tense conversation, and a surprise. We met in a quiet corner of a nearby restaurant and exchanged some small talk as we sat, but soon the Board members asked for my views on the leadership capabilities. I was direct. I said I did not think that John was the right person to lead the business going forward and that we needed to find a replacement, the sooner, the better. The reason, I said, was that, as good as he was performing at the moment, I did not believe he was equipped to alter the direction of the company, scale it, and change it, or deliver the returns we had planned for. I added that many of the company's senior executives shared my misgivings.

You could have heard a pin drop. This did not seem to be what they had expected or wanted to hear. Chris was hearing this for the first time, since we had had no time to discuss my views in advance of the dinner, and he also seemed surprised. In a later discussion, he acknowledged that this was the last thing he had wanted to hear.

Removing a CEO is not to be taken lightly and it is not typically an approach we take at GA. We like to back strong founders and CEOs and support them to grow their businesses and realize our investment objectives. Not surprisingly, after our announcement, there was immediate pushback. We had a thoughtful and well-reasoned discussion over dinner. As a group, we reviewed Hemnet's positive developments. Revenue was growing. Relations with the broker community had improved. And this was not a broken company with dire needs. It was successful.

We unpacked the drivers of past performance and discussed the building blocks that needed to be put in place for the company to hit its strategic goals. One driver from the past had been an increase in listing fees to grow revenues rather than the introduction of new products or other market innovations, or business process updates and margin improvements. But as we looked ahead, different challenges needed to be addressed. These included developing new product lines, improving the website's performance on mobile devices, and a strategy for tackling "technical debt," meaning fixing issues left over from technological upgrades that were important to the sustainability of Hemnet's technology platform but that had been deferred. We needed the organization to be firing on all cylinders to reach its full potential, which would require stronger leadership, clear priorities, and the application of performance management tools. As we wrestled through all this in our conversation, it became obvious that while John had been overseeing a successful business, he was not well-suited to take the business to the next level of growth.

The Board members then asked how we would replace John and what the chances were of finding a good candidate in Sweden, given the relatively small size of the country and talent pool. We acknowledged that finding an experienced consumer technology executive with CEO experience from within Sweden was not going to be easy.

But this was also something that we could not afford to get wrong. Based on our experience at GA involving dozens of companies over several decades, the evidence shows that investment returns are strongly affected by when you change the CEO, and how many times you make such a change. On average, the IRR was 15.7 percent when a single CEO change was made, meaning that the selection was successful and did not need to be reconsidered. When the CEO was changed two or more times, the IRR dropped to 2.8 percent on average. Perhaps even more important, the average IRR jumped to 36.1 percent when the CEO change, if called for, was made within a year of the closing of the investment, compared with 5.5 percent when the change in CEO was made after the first year.

The message could not be clearer. The data reinforces the insight that it is critical to move with speed and solid judgment when contemplating the need to bring in a new CEO at a portfolio company. Decisive, thoughtful action makes an enormous difference in creating value. Based on this research, we knew that we needed to move quickly with Hemnet and to make the right selection the first time.

The Board members then asked, if we moved forward and replaced John, would it be better to let him go immediately and conduct an open search after appointing an interim CEO, or should we leave him in place while starting a confidential search? One Board member worried that Hemnet might seem rudderless if we removed the CEO immediately and felt that it might be safer to leave John in charge while we searched. But, after analyzing this further, we agreed that, given the lack of clear priorities and the number of high-level vacancies, we needed to act with urgency and let the management know we were clear on our approach.

Hemnet had a dominant market position, and it was ripe for monetization. The potential was huge, but it would be realized only if we moved quickly. I also warned that if we waited and tried searching secretly with the CEO in place, the cumbersome process would slow things dramatically.

We wrestled with the choices as it stretched past midnight. The discussion grew heated at times, but there were no politics at play. By the time the night concluded, we had decided to remove the CEO immediately, appoint the CTO as the interim CEO, and begin a search. The next step was to explain our proposal to the broader Board and let the Directors vote. When they met, not long after, they had a spirited discussion and carefully reviewed my findings. They voted to support our plan.

We moved swiftly to select a qualified search firm and develop a search strategy. We interviewed two firms, and decided to work with Russell Reynolds. We also partnered with a consultant who lived in Sweden and understood the talent landscape in the country, as well as the challenges of finding the right person.

Critical, of course, was developing the candidate criteria. We needed to build alignment between the Board and GA. We especially needed to agree on which qualities were non-negotiable and which ones we might, if necessary, compromise on.

We decided our new leader should bring the following experience and competencies:

- Track record of growing a consumer tech business 3× or 4× over four to six years, while simultaneously expanding margins;

- Track record developing and launching new products and lines of business;

- Track record of hiring and building a strong leadership team;

- Proven experience leading a culture transformation to enhance innovation and results orientation; and

- Preferably a Swede or someone with strong knowledge of the Swedish market and culture.

Our list went through four iterations before we finalized our thinking. Our bullseye candidate was or had been a CEO and had experience growing a company. But, if necessary, we would remain open to a first-time CEO who had experience running a business line as a General Manager. The non-negotiables were prior consumer tech and digital marketing experience, as well as proven ability to drive culture transformation.

We moved quickly, and Russell Reynolds came back in about ten days with an initial slate of candidates. Moving forward, Chris quarterbacked the search efforts, and we maintained a weekly cadence to review progress. Part of my focus was working closely with and supporting Chris, who had not directly led a CEO search previously. He had questions about best approaches in interviews and I shared my experience in using a careful, data-driven approach to obtain the best insights.

Within a few weeks, I was meeting those who made it to the shortlist. We eventually narrowed it down to three candidates, two external and one internal—our interim CEO, Hemnet's CTO. We invited the two external candidates to participate in a case study, which would allow us to see them in action. Based on those performances, we found ourselves gravitating toward a highly capable candidate, Cecilia Beck-Friis.

Cecilia was not a sitting CEO, but she had an impressive track record of performance at TV4, a Swedish television network. At TV4, she had successfully grown digital advertising revenues and the subscriber base and led digital product development for the company. She had inherited a dysfunctional team and made a lot of hard personnel decisions. We liked that she moved quickly and decisively in her past roles. She had been promoted multiple times, but eventually left TV4 to set up a virtual reality business.

Everything was heading in the right direction until, just before we planned to make an offer, Chris received a call from Cecilia. She said she had decided to back out of the process and wanted to be removed from consideration. It was a shock, but she said that, having given it more thought, it was not completely clear to her that she would be fully empowered and given the necessary resources by the Board to run Hemnet as she saw fit and to achieve success. She was also torn, she said, about leaving the virtual reality business she was building from scratch. It did not help that the search, which was rigorous to ensure accuracy of hire, was also tedious, leaving her concerned about decision-making at the company.

At this point, we had full conviction that she was the right person to lead Hemnet and we were not prepared to throw in the towel. To alleviate her concerns, we arranged for Bill Ford, the CEO of General Atlantic, to call her directly to better understand her concerns and to assure her that she would have the support and executive powers that she was seeking. Bill also assured her that the Hemnet investment was a priority for General Atlantic and that the team had full confidence in her ability to lead the company. This call seemed to have an immediate positive impact, and Cecilia accepted the offer. The process took 100 days.

Cecilia has turned out to be an outstanding CEO. She has built a strong team and helped the business expand its product portfolio. Hemnet has more than doubled its revenues and profits in just three years. In April 2021, Hemnet successfully completed an IPO on NASDAQ Stockholm. The stock closed on its first day of trading up 54 percent, implying a market capitalization of $2.1 billion, a greater than 10× increase from when General Atlantic first invested. This result was supported by an extremely strong consumer brand, a scarcity of local growth technology assets, and public investor perception that this is the highest quality public classifieds asset globally (trading at a significant multiple premium to all peers) with a strong and diverse management team.

KEY LEARNINGS

HEMNET

RAM CHARAN

"If it ain't broke, don't fix it." This has been the worst wisdom for centuries. Hemnet was not "broken" when GA invested, so many might have said it needed no repairs. This would have been an error. It faced some great opportunities, but, to seize them, it needed some fixes.

- This chapter underscores a key message for leaders. While a company may be doing well currently, it does not mean you have the right leader in place for the future. On paper, the CEO was strong with relevant, global experience, but the company's culture was underperforming. It is important to note the extent to which Anish was engaged. He completed an in-depth career walkthrough, getting granular details around what the CEO had done and how he had done it. He also spoke with over ten other executives and Board members to get a better understanding of how the CEO showed up as a leader and if they had the confidence that he could take the company forward. Ultimately, Anish came to the conclusion that John was a high-quality executive, but wasn't right for the situation.

- Throughout this story, it is notable how Chris Caulkin, the lead deal partner at GA, approached the situation. He sensed that something was not right, and he had the conviction to trust his instinct and engage Anish. He trusted the data that Anish presented to him and eventually made the tough decision to agree to replace the CEO. This took incredible courage, as he had to go back to the Investment Committee just after completing the deal and tell them the company needed a new CEO. You have to make tough decisions at times. Too often, leaders hang on to talent for too long because they are loyal or have performed well in the past. The loyalty needs to be to the business. The company comes first.

- Running an executive search, especially a CEO search, is not easy. The talent pool was limited in a smaller market like Sweden. The team had invested a lot of time making sure that Cecelia was the right candidate, only to be told that she did not want the job. However, Chris had spent the time building the relationship with her throughout the process. They even brought in Bill Ford to get on a call to understand why she was saying no, what concerns she had, and ultimately satisfying those concerns. This perseverance and determination exemplify General Atlantic's commitment and belief that getting the right talent in place is crucial to their investment strategy.

CHAPTER 7

THE IMPORTANCE OF BACKING THE RIGHT LEADER

ARGUS MEDIA

The CEO of Argus Media, whom I will call Robert, got right down to business in my first meeting with him. We were in New York, in the fall of 2016, and General Atlantic had just made its largest single investment up to that time, acquiring a 53 percent stake in Argus, a London-based energy and commodity price consultancy, business intelligence, and information service company. Because of the size of the transaction and the challenges of scaling up a $1 billion company, a lot was on the line.

Robert, Argus's former COO, was expert in detail, and quickly used the time with me to describe his plans taking cost out of the business, implementing price increases, tackling needed talent upgrades in his executive team, and working on compensation and incentives programs. Argus had been performing well under Robert and the company's Executive Chairman, Adrian Binks, its former CEO and guiding spirit. Robert emphasized process, refining all the things that made the company run, whereas Adrian's focus was on the customer and how the company would differentiate itself in the marketplace

The Argus deal was led by Gabriel Caillaux, one of the firm's Co-Presidents, who leads our EMEA portfolio and brings depth in financial services and technology sectors. Gabe had been tracking and building a relationship with Argus for more than seven years, engaging for much of that time with its founding family and the Chairman. Adrian had played a critical role in building the business from its origins as an insider's newsletter focused on the European oil markets to a global information company. With new technologies and globalization disrupting information industries, the timing for making the investment seemed right, and Gabe persuaded the founding family, the largest shareholders, that General Atlantic's desire to help scale the company, upgrade its technology, and add new capabilities was the right approach for building on their legacy.

Increasingly, digital tools and sophisticated data analytics were creating challenges and opportunities for savvy players in information businesses, Gabe reasoned, and Argus was well-positioned to become a leader in the space. Gabe and General Atlantic's other deal partners knew well that it was one thing to formulate a great deal thesis on paper, and quite another to put in place the high-performing team to deliver on the growth thesis and create multiples in value in a four-to-five-year window. As soon as the deal closed, Gabe asked me to develop a leadership and organization strategy for Argus.

I began with Robert in that first two-hour meeting in New York. I already had a sense that most of our deal partners and executives at Argus regarded him as the voice of the future, which seemed promising. I needed to test his thinking, leadership style, and operating rhythm to understand how he would perform over the long term. Robert was clearly a good manager of processes and operations but, I quickly found, he had no shortage of concerns about what he perceived to be roadblocks in his path. But these weren't ordinary roadblocks. They centered on differing visions and a lack of alignment between him and Adrian, the Executive Chairman. Adrian was not only the former CEO before Robert, he was a major shareholder. He owned a substantial stake, which he retained when General Atlantic made its investment.

Robert shared his many frustrations about the lack of alignment with Adrian, explaining that he felt he was handicapped and not being given the autonomy to succeed. He said Adrian often involved himself in operating issues and frequently challenged his decisions related to corporate priorities, talent, and pricing. Robert noted straightforwardly that he expected that Adrian, as Executive Chairman, would oversee activities from 10,000 feet up, offering guidance but leaving the day-to-day management of the business to the CEO. When I asked him what he expected from the partnership with General Atlantic, Robert suggested creating a buffer between him and Adrian.

The key for me, I realized, was to assess the situation during my meeting with Adrian, as well as with other members of the leadership team, and remain open-minded as I gathered information. That this involved the Board Chair and the second-largest shareholder required that I work even more closely with Gabe and his team, and eventually the Argus Board, drawing data-driven conclusions about how we could address the situation and line up the options. Just getting to that conversation with Adrian proved, however, something of a challenge. When I flew to London to spend additional time with Robert and meet Adrian and the broader leadership team, I was surprised that I was scheduled to meet with Adrian for only forty-five minutes, while meetings with the rest of leadership team members were scheduled for ninety minutes each. Fortunately, when I met Adrian, he was warm and graciously said he could go as long as was required. We ended up speaking for nearly three hours.

Adrian, who had been at Argus for more than thirty years, articulated a clear vision for the business. He emphasized that the company needed to build a strong, long-range growth strategy that included expanding in key markets, such as the

US and Asia, aligning its capabilities with global customers, and building new products and analytics capabilities to keep ahead of changing commodities markets. He had joined Argus shortly after it was founded, and he had not only risen to become CEO and Chairman, he was also highly respected for the depth of his knowledge of the energy markets and especially for his relationships with large customers, major oil companies, and traders. Understanding and responding to customer needs was critical in scaling Argus to become a leading competitor to the longtime industry leader, S&P Global Platts.

Adrian was focused on customers, helping them anticipate future market demands and giving them cutting-edge digital tools for analyzing and operating in commodities markets, especially oil. He was strategic and looked outward. In fact, he had hired Robert as his COO in 2010 so that he could focus on the big-picture strategy while allowing Robert to handle process and internal operations. At the time, this was the right move for the organization. Robert's skills as a strong operator complemented Adrian. Robert was efficient and improved processes.

During my conversation with Adrian, I learned that he was committed to continued expansion and growth and felt that, in pursuing a global strategy and by adding new capabilities, the company could grow in value multifold in the next few years.

I met with about twenty other executives at Argus, unpacking each individual's specific responsibilities, priorities, and perceived challenges ahead. I also carefully probed each individual on their perceptions of the divide between Adrian and Robert. The story I heard was consistent. Most of Argus's executives had fallen into one of two camps, one behind Robert and one behind Adrian. Further, the two camps were not communicating or coordinating well with each other. The company, though performing well, was siloed, which was driven largely by a lack of cohesion at the top between Adrian and Robert. Most of the executives, no matter which camp they fell into, expressed uncertainty about whose orders to follow.

Given the sensitivity of our findings, we brought in the leadership consulting firm RHR International to do a deep dive and come up with its own independent assessment. Its findings about the clash and lack of cohesion mirrored our own. Ultimately, we had to ask ourselves: how could we take a $1 billion company and create $3 billion to $4 billion of value with such conflict? And whose vision would best facilitate meeting that objective?

A lot of this conflict, I quickly learned, was a product of the way Robert had come to his position as CEO, which predated GA's investment. Adrian was an exceedingly bright, self-made person from humble origins—his father was a gardener on an English aristocrat's estate before joining the UK's Royal Air Force in the Second World War, after which he went into business; his grandfather was a coal miner who was killed in a roof collapse at his colliery. Adrian went to Cambridge University and then joined the oil industry, with his first job at BP. He began by writing speeches and presentations for senior executives, but after the OPEC oil shocks, starting in the 1970s, he moved into the trading division, where he deepened his knowledge of the markets and the players. He was persuaded to join the tiny UK-owned Argus newsletter in 1984 and bought in as a minority shareholder. Then as oil markets expanded rapidly in both scope and sophistication through the 1990s and 1990s, he became the company's CEO and grew the business enormously.

In 2014, however, Adrian fell ill. The Argus Board, still led by the children of the founder Jan Nasmyth, who had passed away in 2008, felt it needed to ensure consistent leadership in his absence. With Robert lobbying both them and the Independent Directors to give him the CEO job, the Board agreed to do so in June 2015.

When Adrian's health improved, he returned as the Executive Chair, and subsequently GA invested in the business. Robert expected Adrian to disengage from daily operational responsibilities while he held on to the top executive job. Adrian had a strong founder's mentality. Having shepherded Argus for so many years, he had deeper knowledge of the markets and closer relationships with the customers than Robert did. This was useful in helping us understand the source of the difficulties, but we still had to figure out how to resolve the conflict and scale up the business under clear and unified leadership.

For me, the moment when the fog of claims and counterclaims lifted came in a conversation where I asked Robert about his strategic priorities going forward. He mentioned issues such as improving performance management and incentive programs, upgrading talent, and improving operating processes. Two critical issues were conspicuous by their absence—he did not mention customers and he did not describe a forward-looking strategy that would enable Argus to remain a leader in what was a highly competitive and changing marketplace. Robert had many strengths, but he did not bring the same breadth of industry experience that Adrian brought to the table. I also questioned why he didn't move faster to upgrade and strengthen his management team if that was among his top priorities.

I took my findings to Gabe, and we went through an iterative process weighing the pros and cons of both alternatives. Ultimately, it increasingly became clear that Adrian's forte was vision, strategy, and customer relations and that he carried unparalleled knowledge of the sector. It was hard to imagine how we could scale the company without that vision.

After my dialogue with Gabe, all the shareholders, including Adrian, convened. We concluded that the situation with Robert was unresolvable. We all felt that it was in the best interests of both leaders and the company to let Robert go. In hindsight, one strength of this process was that my partners and I had remained open-minded and followed the facts. We were rigorous in collecting data on the two leaders, cross-checked information with other executives, and listened carefully before drawing conclusions. That led us to make what we are now certain was the right move.

As a news article put it in January 2017, "Argus Media chairman Adrian Binks will resume the role of chief executive at the energy news and price reporting agency, eight months after the announcement of its sale to U.S. investment firm General Atlantic, the company said in an internal memo."

What Makes an "A" CEO?

Insights from Senior Leaders at GA
When I joined General Atlantic, I surveyed our most experienced deal partners and asked them what distinguishes a great CEO from an average CEO. A few key themes emerged:

- **Sets Direction:** Has a clear and compelling vision. Makes decisions with speed and conviction, but pauses for decisions that are "high impact and irreversible."

- **Keeps Customers at the Core:** Immerses into the customer's experience and always considers customer satisfaction and retention.

- **Builds & Energizes Org:** Leads with integrity. Builds "A" teams and makes tough decisions. Builds a culture of extreme collaboration.

- **Drives Execution:** Prioritizes and aligns resources and drives radical accountability. Integrates Strategy, Talent & Operating Plan.

But that still left us with an open position. We launched a search for a high-quality leader who could assume the role of a COO, provide leverage to Adrian, and, under his mentorship, get to know the market and major customers.

Adrian, Gabe, and I started by discussing the COO search criteria, and we remained joined at the hip during the search. We needed to make certain that we were all aligned on the skills and experiences that would be required in the role. We knew it would be imperative to target someone with a strong track record of growing businesses and strengthening technology, and had proven enterprise-wide leadership. Perhaps most important, we had to make certain we would be selecting someone who could work collaboratively with Adrian. After considering several firms, we chose Heidrick & Struggles to lead the search.

We met with many qualified candidates and eventually narrowed it to four finalists. We met with each of them multiple times, for up to three hours in a session. One who checked all the right boxes and seemed to have the right personality for fitting in and working with Adrian was Matthew Burkley. He had successfully built several businesses, including one he had founded, so he understood the challenges of scaling a business and had demonstrated strong entrepreneurial energy.

At that time, he was the CEO of another information business, Genscape, which provides real-time data and analytics on commodities and energy markets. He had tripled the company's size in six years, proving his ability to expand a business securely. He had strong strategic acumen and had experience growing businesses within Thomson Reuters, so he understood both the energy and information sectors and the technology behind them. While relatively young, he was intellectually strong and technically competent, already had a strong track record, and had experience in entrepreneurial and corporate environments. Not least, he knew Argus well and was excited about its prospects.

As we narrowed our list of finalists, we invited Matthew and another promising candidate to participate in a case study exercise so that we could observe them in action and test their understanding of the business. We provided both candidates with company and financial material and asked them to prepare and deliver forty-five-minute presentations to the search committee, which was followed by forty-five minutes of questions and discussion. Both performed impressively, but Matthew had the edge, in part because of the warm relationship he seemed to be developing with Adrian.

The critical question was if he would be willing to join as COO and work under Adrian, who would be both CEO and Chairman. One of the other finalists had opted out of the process because of that condition. Matthew was self-aware as a leader, and did not seem the type to let ego get in his way. He said he understood both the great opportunity Argus presented and the strengths Adrian brought to the business. I spoke with Adrian and said I was concerned that Matthew, like the other candidate, still might decline if not given the CEO title. Adrian suggested that he take Matthew to lunch and have a frank talk. To our delight, Adrian sealed the deal and we hired Matthew as COO in September 2017.

Still, we were careful to make sure from the start that we did not allow divisions to take root and that we laid out a foundation for constructive collaboration. Adrian created a new office configuration, placing Matthew and himself in glass offices facing each other so there was, quite literally, transparency. Each could see what the other was doing and who they were meeting. They jointly attended key meetings. The setup engendered greater trust and alignment, and helped ensure that they were pursuing a common agenda. The system has been a great success.

Within the first month there, Matthew ran an aggressive performance management program and used it to replace lower-performing managers and strengthen leadership deeper in the organization. Adrian and he moved quickly to build out Argus's senior leadership capabilities, which included promoting the former US country leader into a global business unit role, and later appointing an internal leader into a newly created Chief Commercial Officer role to oversee sales and marketing on a global scale. With our support, Argus hired a new CTO and CHRO, and has since hired a new global head of Editorial and a leader for the oil business in the US, and has reorganized or replaced much of its regional management to create a more globally focused business.

Additionally, Adrian and Matthew worked in tandem and moved quickly to restructure the organization, creating business units with the intent of pushing P&L accountability deeper into the organization. Leaders of each unit now own their respective P&L and customer relationships.

Backing Adrian as CEO and hiring Matthew as COO has proved to be the right strategy, evidenced by the company's exceptional performance over the past four years. Under their collective leadership, Argus's top and bottom line have continued to grow in the double digits annually, and the business has created over $2 billion in value since our initial investment.

KEY LEARNINGS

ARGUS MEDIA

RAM CHARAN

Nothing is more devastating in the creation of market cap than misalignment in the two top people, be it the Chair and the CEO or the founder and the CEO or a CEO and COO. It can be toxic. It is the largest energy drainer in the corporation from the top to the bottom. In Argus, we see Anish and his team identifying this promptly. This is an area many can make blunders. They could choose the wrong person, they could fire both people, and they could waste time to recruit new people.

- When deciding on a CEO, or any key executive of a business, you must start with a set of standards that defines what an "A" leader would look like. This is the framework by which anyone who is interviewed should be assessed. In the case of the CEO, having a deep understanding of the customer and where the markets are moving is critical. Without the customer, there is no business. A high-quality CEO must also have a strategic vision for the company and use that vision to set direction for their team. This framework is what allowed Gabe, Adrian, and Anish to make the correct decision, the one that has led Argus to create over $2 billion in market cap.

- As soon as you know a change needs to be made, you need to act decisively. There are, of course, times when you should pause and reflect, especially on changes that are permanent and have a high impact. But once you have landed on that decision, speed is critical. This was crucial in the case of Argus. In less than a year, Adrian reassumed CEO duties and the COO search was kicked off. Adrian, Gabe, and Anish quickly aligned on the search criteria and hit the ground running. Any delay in this process could have resulted in a delay in hitting the investment targets.

- There are no shortcuts when running a search. You must do the diligence and meet with multiple candidates multiple times in different settings to be assured that you're selecting the right leader. You can have candidates participate in case studies, which has the benefit of not only seeing them in action, but also getting them more familiar and excited about the company and its prospects for the future. Once the right leader is on board, you must set them up for success. Build trust, create transparency, and collaborate with your new leader. This is how you foster a lasting working relationship and create alignment in pursuing a common goal.

.

CHAPTER 8

BUILDING A LEADERSHIP TEAM FOR A SUCCESSFUL MERGER

HIRERIGHT

Guy Abramo took over as the CEO of General Information Services, or GIS, in early 2018. He brought a lot of dynamism and energy to the role. He had been president of the consumer business at Experian and had worked many years in technology and data management businesses, but this was his first shot at holding a CEO position and working for a private equity-backed company. It was also an important opportunity for General Atlantic, which had invested in GIS in 2017 after a long search for good opportunities in the pre-employment background verification industry.

Since 2014, my General Atlantic partners, led by Peter Munzig, had been studying a critical new reality in corporate life, the accelerated mobility of executives and staff between jobs. This human capital revolution had been rippling through the business world, in the process affecting numerous aspects of the pre-employment background verification process. Background checks, in particular, are no longer the sleepy routines they had once typically been. People may have five jobs before turning thirty these days, and many more in the years after; each time someone makes a move, the companies need to review voluminous numbers of job candidates to make certain they are hiring capable talent.

That is an especially sensitive concern today, since employee problems and employee conflicts, if they surface publicly, can crackle through social media channels, staining reputations and embarrassing businesses. So, at General Atlantic, Peter had locked in on trying to invest in one of the companies that perform the essential service of background checks, which includes looking into criminal records, driving records, drug testing, employment and education verification, and industry-specific compliance and screening requirements. GIS, then the fourth largest in the industry and based in a small town in South Carolina, had responded to a cold call from Peter, engaged in a lengthy series of conversations, and became our successful foray into the sector. General Atlantic acquired a large minority stake from the founder in March 2017.

We had had some near misses before that, but in GIS we felt we had found a company with a long and steady record, a solid customer base, and, importantly, a platform that we could scale up to multiply the value of our investment. It's a high-margin industry and customer relationships tend to be relatively long term, so we felt good about the prospects. Also, it was a fragmented industry, with many capable, smaller companies, so from the start we were thinking of opportunities for consolidation, not just organic growth. But there was much we needed to learn as we explored and evaluated GIS.

We swiftly got a taste of reality. We found that the company, still controlled by its founder, was performing reasonably well, but was not ready for the rigors of rapid expansion; it needed some critical upgrades to meet our deal objectives. That was not a great surprise, since most companies are outfitted and managed for where they are in the marketplace at any given moment, rather than where they hope to be in two or three years. The founder, who was still the majority shareholder, had hired a new CEO, but, once we looked at the business's challenges, we agreed we needed someone with more in-depth technology experience and the ability to institute operating improvements to get the company ready for rapid growth. That launched a lengthy search process that resulted in the hiring of Guy, a tech-savvy and data-oriented leader.

We were confronting a central issue in General Atlantic's talent management process, which arises in many of our portfolio investments at one time or another. When we scale businesses, they not only grow but they change. The leaders need to be farsighted, capable of both driving and managing change, eager to adopt innovations and delegate key responsibilities to the team members, and clear on holding executives accountable and moving swiftly to replace those who do not possess the skills to realize performance goals. My assessment methodology is built around recognizing patterns for what will prove successful and what needs support and coaching or replacing. This was key in our GIS search and in my efforts to support my partners in transforming the investment.

Guy, our choice for CEO, was proactive and results-driven, and quickly gathered information on GIS once he took over, assessing its leadership, its challenges, and how he could start scaling it up in line with General Atlantic's deal thesis. He came to some sobering conclusions quickly.

Within ten days of doing his own deep dive, Guy found a company that, in key respects, was coasting, with a long list of impediments to its ultimate success. It had attracted no major new clients in several years, and it was slowly losing some clients. It was a sales-led organization, with a high-touch sales organization but weak technology. That was important, since the key to growth and expansion around the globe would be having an effective platform to provide better and faster service to customers. Technology was

GIS's Achilles' heel. The Chief Information Officer did not seem to be up to leading the required upgrades. Overall, the company's organization and operations lacked the maturity of a global, high-volume business.

After a month, Guy discussed his views with Peter and the General Atlantic team. He told them that, in his view, they either needed to invest many millions right away into major technology upgrades and stronger leadership for several functions, a potentially time-consuming process, or they should consider what Peter had long contemplated, finding a merger partner that brought scale and a global platform. No one wanted to lose a year or more in an uncertain rebuilding process, so they agreed that the most attractive option seemed to be finding a partner.

Peter already knew the industry and the players well, so he was able to assess potential acquisitions quickly and put out some feelers. He found a strong candidate, HireRight, a major player in the industry. With roots in the early 1980s and growth from its own acquisitions over the years, HireRight was the third largest in the business. Now, its owners were struggling with difficulties that, fortunately, had no connection with HireRight's operations. That presented an opportunity to acquire the company, even though it was larger than GIS.

After a competitive process, General Atlantic acquired what became a 52 percent stake in the company created by the merger of GIS and HireRight. The merger was completed in just a few months, in July 2018, and the newly enlarged business's headquarters was moved from South Carolina to Irvine, California, where HireRight had been based. That instantly made it much easier to recruit new talent.

HireRight had an excellent client base, with several of the world's largest companies. It was growing and it had a better technology platform than GIS. It was also a respected brand in the industry. General Atlantic's philosophy is focused on creating value by scaling up promising companies, but, in this case, we found that we could also remove significant costs by eliminating redundancies and finding synergies as we merged the systems at GIS and HireRight. We targeted and reduced costs by about $30 million a year.

It was a promising start, and Guy quickly called a big gathering of the executive ranks of the newly merged company, which we called HireRight, in Newport Beach, California. Guy wanted to meet his leadership team, strengthen morale and collaboration, and begin establishing and articulating priorities. But as he prepared to address the group for the first time, Guy had his second shock since becoming CEO. He looked out, he recalled to me later, at what was a sea of unhappy faces. It was an obvious mix of doubt and disgust. He had never confronted that kind of open hostility, but the HireRight executives did not hide their concern about being acquired by the smaller GIS, a company they felt was not as strong or of the same caliber as the old HireRight. The challenges of meshing the two different organizations and creating a unified, more technologically innovative business suddenly looked more daunting.

As he dug in, Guy found that the HireRight he inherited also had some critical operational shortcomings and leadership needs that could impede the scaling process. The technological infrastructure was fragmented, with three systems that would have to be upgraded and merged—one for healthcare companies, another for international clients, and a core platform. Making it more difficult, they had just invested more than $20 million in a new data center, when, Guy found, they could have done it cheaper and better by transitioning to a cloud-based system. Guy also felt they needed to significantly top-grade their leadership team.

The current Human Resources Officer worked remotely, in New York, so she had little direct contact with the employees in Irvine and elsewhere, a decided problem for a business with 3,000 employees. There were few effective performance tracking systems in place to evaluate the management. Guy decided he would have to bring in a new CHRO to work on-site, which was also an opportunity to transform and upgrade the position to elevate the importance of talent development and management at the company. Guy found that the middle management ranks at HireRight had lots of excellent talent. That was helpful, but Guy believed that a critical overall problem was that the executives and leadership teams did not have the knowledge or experience needed to scale up the business, and possibly not the desire.

In late 2018, Peter asked me to do a thorough leadership and organizational assessment of HireRight, develop a clearer picture of its needs, and prepare a plan to get it on track.

This included a leadership team assessment, an examination of the short- and long-term priorities, recommendations on where they needed talent upgrades, assessments of the organizational structure and operating rhythm, and a broad look at employee morale. It was a demanding job, but the findings from this assessment would help ensure that Guy had the right priorities, and our support, for this difficult phase of his work.

There was also a critical question we had to help Guy confront. He told us he had a concern that if he tackled too many of the company's shortcomings at once, from replacement of executives to a reorganization, he could break the business and cause a paralysis in the management. Our assessment, we hoped, would give him the confidence he needed and let him know how he should pace the transformation.

Perhaps more important, we had to analyze if Guy, as good as he had been at bringing some stability to the business after the merger, now attending to operational details and instilling greater focus on his priorities, was the right person to lead HireRight as we scaled up and could manage the company we expected it to be in three years, when it would be much larger and more international.

We began by assessing all the members of the leadership, and found mixed results by the time we finished in March 2019. We affirmed Guy's judgment that they needed key talent upgrades in areas such as technology, human resources, revenue growth, and sales. Guy himself looked strong as an operating leader.

Overall, the feedback on Guy was positive. His team had confidence that he was the right CEO to take the company forward. However, we also held up a mirror and quoted back to him some of the critical comments from his team, so he understood that this was useful and candid feedback, and laid out our recommendations in a debriefing that stretched to nearly three hours. He knew that we had spent up to more than two hours with most of his executives and had hundreds of pages of notes in our data-driven analysis. Different CEOs respond differently to feedback, with some resenting it, but Guy quickly embraced our insights. He appreciated the support and opportunities to develop, and the resources that General Atlantic brought.

One of our insights was that, given the weakness of the leadership team, Guy was increasingly pulled into granular operational issues. His pace was fast, and he was intensively involved in the day-to-day matters. We felt he needed to upgrade and cut the number of direct reports by about half. Guy felt he needed to be deeply immersed because of the precarious nature of the business as the merger moved forward, but we explained that his close-in operating style meant he devoted far too little time to bigger strategic goals.

He needed to create leverage, delegating more responsibility to his team, and ensuring there was a system to hold them accountable for performance. That would free more of his time to develop bigger objectives for the business, such as developing the product platform, investing time into key client meetings, and working on international expansion. In addition, if we were to take HireRight public, he would need to carve out even more of his time toward public company matters.

A massive transition was underway at HireRight. We had combined two companies, leaving some managers unhappy, though most seemed to appreciate Guy's strengths as the CEO. The company was generally performing, but we did not yet have either the right organizational structure or the operating rhythm that we knew was needed to multiply value as planned. We had to make some key hires and work on the technology upgrades.

And we had to think about the culture. I knew that both Guy and Peter had concerns about not trying to force too much change by injecting multiple new leaders too fast on an already stressed system. But I concluded that there was more risk in having mediocre talent in key positions than in moving forward. There was no need to hold back. The more we waited, the more time would be lost and the more challenging it would be to scale up and achieve our goals for the increase in value.

I based my assessment on three key business priorities: revenue growth, developing a global tech platform, and building an efficient operations infrastructure.

To achieve these priorities, we needed a Chief Revenue Officer, Chief Product Officer, and Operations Head. Perhaps most importantly, we also needed a CHRO who could not only provide support on these searches, but could help Guy knit together a strong leadership team, assimilate and onboard new leaders, and drive a high-performing culture. A high-quality CHRO could have a significant impact on business performance and strengthen collaboration across functions.

We supported Guy in his search for the CHRO. The choice, and the way it has worked, reaffirmed and deepened my own view of the new model of the role. The CHRO should be a key driver of overall corporate performance, not an isolated administrator operating in a silo.

Guy agreed we needed a CHRO who would do more than administer a series of discrete employee functions. He wanted a trusted adviser, a collaborator, ensuring that he communicated well with his team and supported them sufficiently. He wanted someone who would act as the glue within his team, making certain that they understood one another and were well-synchronized in their pursuit of major strategic objectives, exchanged information efficiently, and were held accountable for performance.

Guy took almost six months to whittle the candidates to four finalists. All were accomplished, but Guy was drawn to the youngest and least experienced, a woman, Chelsea Pyrzenski, who had previously been at VIZIO and had played an important role in fostering successful change management at DIRECTV. He felt that they had a stronger chemistry, that she would be candid in her assessments, and that she could break free from the old model of an HR leader.

In fact, she has transformed the role, devoting less time to the traditional administrative functions of Human Resources and more time on ensuring better communication and cohesion in the leadership team, tracking performance, strengthening talent development and building talent pipelines, and transforming the role into a key business partner of the leadership team rather than as a cost center. All that has enhanced Chelsea's effectiveness. She replaced and upgraded about two-thirds of the HR staff, developed new employee compensation programs, and now monitors employee engagement regularly.

Chelsea pursued her job with a clear sense of the changes she needed to instill in Guy's team. That started with her efforts to build trust. She needed to persuade the executives that she was an unbiased listener and not just a pipeline to Guy. Her focus, she made clear, was successful business performance, and she was adept at assisting the executives in enhancing their contributions and meeting objectives. That gave her credibility and improved their trust.

Chelsea spent time working with Guy in building out a collaborative and cohesive team. When executives shared their concern that meetings tended to be brief and too narrowly focused on specific agenda items, she worked with Guy to loosen up the agendas and create more time for deeper discussions on key business priorities and for problem solving. Not surprisingly, there were differences at times between what Guy believed he was communicating and what his team felt they had heard. Chelsea was able to explain these differences to Guy and help him understand how he could express his thoughts more effectively to get buy-in from his team and strengthen the sense of ownership.

Chelsea emphasized strengthening the talent deeper in the organization. She partnered with each of the leadership team members to identify the critical roles in their function, identify potential gaps and areas for development, and develop a strategy to attract and retain talent for those roles. In particular, she supported the CRO, CTO, and CPO in upgrading the talent in their functions.

She also worked actively in building out and improving the culture of the organization. She worked with Guy to improve communications, making sure that the company strategy, priorities, mission, and vision were properly conveyed and understood. Because of this, eNPS scores have improved by 33 percent since she joined the company. Confidence in the leadership team has gone up, people feel they have the resources and tools to do their job, and transparency has improved.

It is typical for the CHRO to spend a dominant percent of their time focused internally. I think it's highly likely that future CHROs will need to be more externally oriented, benchmarking people and organizational capabilities at competitors, proactively building talent pools, and learning how to leverage talent that lives beyond the boundaries of their organization. The more that CHROs can free themselves up from the administrative HR role and instead focus on building talent and organizational capabilities behind mission-critical priorities, the better off the business would be.

In 2019, the company finished building out the core platform and migrated its customers to it. They built out capabilities in sales and marketing, leading to a record first quarter in 2020. The Covid pandemic affected the business as the economy contracted and hiring slowed down. Guy sensed the changes coming and moved exceptionally fast to right-size the organization, maintaining margins, but at the same time built out capabilities to acquire more and better customers. In conversations with the Board, we found that Guy demonstrated great leadership and confidence throughout the year and brought his team together. By improving communications during Covid, ensuring the safety of employees, and focusing on organizational well-being, employee morale continued to improve. HireRight is poised to continue its accelerated expansion, and is expecting double-digit growth.

KEY LEARNINGS

HIRERIGHT

RAM CHARAN

When your business doesn't have the capabilities you require to scale and multiply value, you need to be creative. In the case of HireRight, this was a merger of two businesses, but even more complex, this was a smaller company buying a larger one. This story brings to light the importance of moving quickly, the role of the CHRO, and the necessity of building out the right team to help a CEO, and company, thrive.

- A few months after the merger, Peter Munzig and Guy came to Anish saying there would be value in developing a talent strategy for the company. Given the complexity of the merger, there was a risk that moving too fast could break down the company, but if they didn't move fast enough, they would never achieve the investment objectives. Guy fully understood this. He moved incredibly fast, was results-driven, and pulled all the right value creation levers. He took on mission impossible of rebuilding four platforms and migrating onto a single platform within twelve months and delivered.

- Peter and the Board knew that HireRight had the potential to be a public company. This meant that

Guy needed to be surrounded with leaders who could provide him leverage so that he could not only get out of the weeds and be more strategic, but also potentially transition to a public company CEO. Public company CEOs need that leverage, as up to 20 percent of their time will be dedicated to public company matters. Guy found the right leaders that he could delegate to instead of constantly running 100 miles per hour.

- You can be a CHRO who can affect the market cap of your company without having a long history of CHRO experience. Guy hired a young talent in Chelsea who he felt could drive the change that the organization needed. What made Chelsea so great is that she got the executives on the leadership team to hone in on critical areas of work that the CEO wanted them to focus on and ensured follow-through on those decisions. Chelsea broke free from the typical CRHO mold, devoting less of her time on administrative matters and instead focusing on building trust among the leadership team, ensuring that the team was working together effectively and communicating well with each other. By doing that, she freed up time for the CEO to invest in higher-impact items. The hallmark of a successful CHRO is making contributions to business performance that are visible and measurable.

CHAPTER 9

CONCLUSION

It is no surprise that the right talent in the right roles multiplies market cap. This has not changed for centuries, it is not changing now, and will not change in the future. But then why do some people fail and some succeed brilliantly? Why do some succeed in the short term and fail in the long term? Few succeed in both. Therein lies the secret that the Right Talent Model is not just a process. Leveraging talent for value creation requires an overhaul of traditional HR practices to increase accountability and focus on critical talent decisions. I had the opportunity to learn, design and implement this philosophy throughout my career. How did I get here?

One of my critical formative professional experiences took place shortly after I joined Novartis International AG, the pharmaceutical company, in 2000. I sat down with our charismatic CEO, Daniel Vasella, shortly after I started as the company's head of talent, to discuss my priorities and plans. After we chatted briefly, he jumped to what was clearly, for him, a nagging question expressed as an observation. "I have 200,000 employees," he said, "but I don't know where the talent is."

His point was striking and, I'm certain, familiar to many CEOs of large enterprises: it's easy to get headcount data on employees and résumé details, but it's exceedingly difficult to identify the true high potentials deeper in the business. Dan recognized that the future of Novartis, its ability to adapt to and excel in a highly competitive, rapidly changing marketplace, depended on his being able to identify and develop those promising leaders, but he did not have the right tools or the data to do it.

That was a powerful statement about the state of human capital management, and Dan made it clear he needed better systems for ensuring he had not just the right numbers of competent people in appropriate seats but high-potential talent, constantly nurtured and challenged, to innovate and drive Novartis' growth. He tasked me with redefining the company's talent programs and building a pipeline of future leaders to deliver superior performance.

This mandate and my experience at Novartis have had a profound impact on my professional career and my guiding philosophy. Dan felt Novartis had been overindexing on hiring externally for senior roles and needed to build a strong internal talent pipeline to support his audacious goals. Dan said he did not want an occasional strong year; he wanted every year to produce performance records, and he needed superior talent and a strong talent engine to achieve that.

At Novartis, I worked closely with division CEOs and enlisted high-potential individuals in the company to help develop a curriculum of talent programs that would have both short- and long-term impact on performance. During my time there, we developed an approach that helped the entire organization "talk talent" in a unified and consistent way, and developed numerous programs for identifying, mentoring, and developing high-potential talent. The methodical grooming process that we developed dramatically strengthened the skills of participants in the programs, boosted morale, and gave us a solid bench of talent that we could draw from to fill key positions.

The talent strategy we developed had broad impact on the company and its performance. When we started the program, roughly 70 percent of open senior management positions were filled externally. The programs we implemented helped us flip that percentage, and allowed us to start filling a majority of those positions with internal candidates.

Word got around. Over the years, those who had gone through our accelerated development and CEO mentoring program were, not surprisingly, much sought after by other companies seeking high-performing talent. At least eighteen of the program's participants went on to be hired as CEOs at other companies, turning Novartis into something of a CEO factory.

Those experiences helped shape my view that talent is a central engine of value creation, a value creator that separates mediocre from strong businesses. It is not always easy to stay focused on this truth in the midst of the complex daily grind that comes with running high-growth organizations.

This same philosophy is deeply embedded at General Atlantic, and articulated by our CEO, Bill Ford, regularly. The GA Talent Playbook has proven its value repeatedly. The case studies you have read exemplify how this methodology works in the rough-and-tumble of daily life. These case studies also illustrate that selecting superior talent is critical, but it is just as important to have the right incentives and the right environment for them to excel. As both Bill Ford & Alex Gorsky stressed in our conversations, growth CEOs build high-quality teams. They regularly re-calibrate and work to raise their bar on talent, and evaluate their leaders, not just on how well they performed in the past, but how well they are positioned to untangle tomorrow's challenges. They put the business first and are willing to part ways with previously high-performing executives when they do not fulfill the needs required for future growth.

Importantly, another critical quality of an effective growth CEO is self-awareness. High-quality leaders understand their strengths as well as their limitations, they understand how the business must evolve to seize new opportunities, and are eager to embrace new ideas. As a high-potential CEO, this was one of the most impressive characteristics of the CEO of Oak Street Health, Mike Pykosz. Mike and his other cofounders came from the world of consulting and had limited operational experience. Mike understood that. The first time we met in a General Atlantic conference room, he expressed delight that I was available to support him in developing his leadership team and talent strategy. CEOs can be reluctant to receive advice, but Mike was enthusiastic and open. I told him that he should never underplay investing in his development, and he hasn't. The CEO needs to grow as fast as the company, and stay ahead.

As I look at the current economic environment, I believe strategic talent management is going to become significantly more important over the next few years as the battered US and global economies emerge from the trauma and tragedy of the COVID-19 pandemic. In the new era we are confronting, which undoubtedly will be a journey of setbacks as well as exceptional opportunities, finding innovative ways to attract and retain high-performing talent will be the engine of value creation, the difference between mediocrity and superior performance.

Current economic conditions are likely to bring this even more into focus. I start with the view that we expect that consumption, crushed under the weight of the shutdown, may well explode as government stimulus measures take hold, vaccination rates rise, and infection rates drop. As we have already seen, every level of economic activity has been impacted. Supply chains will be stressed, creating enormous management challenges. Nimble, imaginative, disciplined talent will make the difference and perhaps determine which businesses can take advantage of the expansion.

In the words of Martin Escobari, Co-President and Chairman of our Investment Committee: "Global dislocations created by the pandemic are just one example of the accelerated pace of disruption facing businesses globally. We have seen the benefits of global integration and disruptive technologies, but they also bring about new risks. The diffusion of disruptive events (like the pandemic) or technologies (like social media or distributed finance) can dramatically change a firm's competitive position overnight. To prepare for a world where chaos hits more frequently, firms will need to evolve. Successful evolution requires a new talent strategy."

As a result, the War for Talent will only get more intense. Proven leaders with demonstrated records of high performance are going to be pursued as never before. It will be more difficult, and more expensive, to recruit and retain them.

The objective previously, especially for conservative business thinkers, was to find candidates who had already done the jobs being filled, executives with proven experience, giving them a false sense of security. As the bidding for talent becomes more competitive and the pace of innovation and disruption continues to increase, leaders will need to learn to hire, retain, and develop talent that has potential to scale.

In other words, businesses will have to make bets on potential. This means they will have to be skilled at evaluating talent and recognizing promise that may not have fully blossomed.

Building a strong leadership team will continue to be critical for business performance, which means that companies will need to develop strength in recruiting with a focus on speed and accuracy, but they will also need to plan and prepare a solid pipeline of talent inside the company. Some of the best recruits will have to be sourced internally, which means companies will need systematic programs, similar to what I developed at Novartis, for identifying those people and grooming them so they are ready when important opportunities open.

And this talent cannot be a carbon copy of the leaders who came before. In the knowledge economy impacting all areas of our lives, business leaders need a broader range of skills than previously required to deliver multiples in value creation. In the globally networked world, organizations must collaborate more than ever, internally as well as with other organizations and partners, across boundaries and across disciplines. Future generations of leaders must be more agile and comfortable with ambiguity and be able to anticipate and build capabilities ahead of the curve. They are going to need to learn at a much faster pace than ever before and be the drivers of innovation and change.

As the qualities that define a great leader evolve, so too will the qualities that define a great team. Leadership teams will be more distributed and diverse, which in turn will require rewriting the rules of engagement. Teams will need to be more fluid and bring complementary experiences and skills as well as different perspectives and backgrounds.

To be successful, companies need to start preparing for that now, recognizing the critical role of talent management in the value chain and how that imperative is evolving.

Get your playbooks ready!

ACKNOWLEDGEMENTS

Ram and I are so fortunate to have been exposed to so many great leaders over the years that we have learned from. Each of their unique stories has shaped our own views as business leaders and formed our view that talent is the true value multiplier. All are value creators for their organizations, and we are deeply grateful to have been given the opportunity to work closely with each of them.

We would also like to personally thank all the individuals who were so generous with their time, support, and insights in the creation of this book. At Oak Street Health: Mike Pykosz. At Depop: Maria Raga. At Vishal Retail: Gunender Kapur. At TPG Capital: Puneet Bhatia. At Johnson & Johnson: Alex Gorsky. At Hemnet: Cecilia Beck-Friis. At Argus Media: Adrian Binks. At HireRight: Guy Abramo and Chelsea Pyrzenski.

I'm also immensely grateful to my partners at General Atlantic. Without their conviction and belief that talent is the true market cap multiplier, this book would not have been possible. They have embraced our efforts and have fostered a sense of collaboration and partnership in the truest sense of the words. This is driven by the dedication and focus that Bill Ford has put on talent and he has embedded this into General Atlantic's DNA. Additionally, I would like to thank the partners who provided their support on this book including: Steven Denning, Robbert Vorhoff, Melis Kahya, Chris Caulkin, Gabriel Caillaux, Peter Munzig, Martin Escobari, Anton Levy, Frank Brown, Mike Gosk, Kelly Pettit, and Mary Armstrong.

I also offer thanks to some of my other partners at General Atlantic and other business leaders from whom I have learned so much and who have been a source of great inspiration to me. The list includes: David Hodgson, Aaron Goldman, Paul Stamas, Graves Tompkins, Alex Crisses, Tanzeen Syed, Kell Reilly, Sandeep Naik, Shantanu Rastogi, Justin Sunshine, Brett Zbar, Andy Crawford, Andrew Ferrer, Shaw Joseph, Joern Nikolay, Christian Figge, Luis Cervantes, Eric Zhang, Lefei Sun, Preston McKenzie, David Buckley, Justin Kotzin, Cory Eaves, Alok Misra, Rob Perez, Lu Wang, Gary Reiner, Achim Berg, Ashok Singh, Thomas Ebeling, Norman Walker, Ken DiPietro, Neil Anthony, Abilio Gonzalez, Mahendra Swarup, Bob Swan, Michel Orsinger, Jeff Raikes, Steve Schneider, Jim Williams, Jin-Goon Kim, Sid Kaul, Ludwig Hantson, and Dan Vasella.

We also acknowledge the great contributions of James Sterngold and thank him for making our idea for this book a reality. With Jim's deep experience and skills, his writing helped give shape to the case studies, drew out the key lessons, and transformed facts, anecdotes, and history into compelling narratives that any reader can pick up and understand.

Merrill Perlman provided great editorial support, helping to professionalize the content, and she was an absolute pleasure to work with.

Rohit Bhargava of Ideapress Publishing and Mark Fortier and Nick Davies of Fortier Public Relations have all been crucial to getting this book to the finish line and out to publication.

I also acknowledge my team at General Atlantic, who each have contributed to the success of General Atlantic and its investments and have pushed me to be the best version of myself as a leader. Special thanks go to Alex Stahl and Lindsay Bedard, who have been supporting me throughout this process and provided invaluable guidance and feedback on this book. Thanks, too, to other members of my team at General Atlantic, including Asha Krishnan, Annah Jamison, Asel Ashergold, and Claire Hogg.

Ram and I owe thanks to Cynthia Burr and Geri Willigan at Charan Associates as well as Whitney Foreman at General Atlantic, who managed the project's complex logistics with care and attention to detail.

Finally, and perhaps most important, I want to thank my extended family including my Mom, Dad and my brother,

Rajnish, who more than anyone else instilled the value in me to strive for excellence. I want to thank Dr. KL Chadha and Mohit. Finally and perhaps most important, I want to thank my sons Archit & Arnesh and my wife, Mona, who stayed by my side as we traveled around the world and back. A lifelong partner makes both the journey and destination worthwhile.